BUSINESS PURPOSE AND PERFORMANCE

BUSINESS PURPOSE AND PERFORMANCE

Selections from Talks and Papers by

FREDERICK R. KAPPEL

CHAIRMAN OF THE BOARD
AMERICAN TELEPHONE AND TELEGRAPH COMPANY

DUELL, SLOAN AND PEARCE • New York

First edition

Affiliate of
MEREDITH PRESS
Des Moines & New York

Library of Congress Catalogue Card Number: 64-18475

MANUFACTURED IN THE UNITED STATES OF AMERICA FOR MEREDITH PRESS

FOREWORD

IT WAS suggested that it might be useful to Bell System people, and perhaps to others interested in our enterprise, if some of the remarks I have made in the past several years were brought together in one place.

I agreed mainly because I think there is value in putting a point of view on the record, where anyone can see it if he wishes.

As in any collection of papers that deal in large measure with the goals and problems of a business, certain ideas will be found emphasized more than once; but this in itself may help to reflect the point of view.

All these talks have been abridged from the original, and in a few instances only brief excerpts have been selected. However, editing has been limited to abbreviating the material; substance has not been changed.

FREDERICK R. KAPPEL

CONTENTS

A General View of the Bell System

A GENERAL VIEW OF THE BELL SYSTEM

Adapted from articles that appeared originally in *The Christian Science Monitor* in 1958 *

When I ask people outside of our business what they think the goals of the telephone company ought to be, they make practical, down-to-earth answers.

Give us good service, they say, at reasonable prices. Be human and considerate in your dealings. Play fair with employees and share owners and bondholders. Look ahead—be progressive. Don't ever be complacent or self-satisfied.

These are plain, uncomplicated ideas. They are also pretty far-reaching. To my mind the success of the Bell Telephone System will mostly depend on how well we live by such ideas, and also on how well the public understands that this is what we are trying to do.

Organization

Before I go further, a brief summary of our organization may be helpful. I think too that it will point up an interesting contrast.

The Bell System is a group of companies which provide telephone service in every state. The name "Bell" is applied to the whole group in honor of Alexander Graham Bell, who invented the telephone in 1876. In the group are some twenty-one "operating companies," as we call them, each providing service within its territory.

The American Telephone and Telegraph Company owns all or a majority of the stock of these operating companies and maintains a central staff to help all the companies co-ordinate their

* Figures have been brought up to date as of early 1964.

efforts on common problems. It also builds and operates a nationwide network of long distance lines, interconnecting the territories of the regional companies, and provides service over radiotelephone and submarine cable systems to countries overseas. A. T. & T. likewise owns the Western Electric Company, which manufactures and supplies equipment for the Bell System, and jointly with Western Electric it owns the Bell Telephone Laboratories, which does research work for all the Bell companies.

The Bell System does not by any means provide all telephone service in the United States. Several thousand other companies, large and small, operate telephone exchanges in all sections of the country. Their lines connect with ours so that you can telephone anywhere.

However the Bell System directly serves more than sixty-nine million of the country's eighty-five million telephones. To do this it employs about 740,000 men and women. Also, more than 2,300,000 people have invested savings in A. T. & T. stock, and this is the financial foundation of our ability to serve. The total physical facilities of the Bell System—local and long distance lines, switchboards, dial apparatus, buildings, telephone instruments, and all other equipment—represent an investment of more than twenty-five billion dollars.

This brings me to the contrast I mentioned.

A Business Both Nationwide and Local

Ours is plainly a very big business. In fact, in dollars invested, abundance of physical plant, number of employees, and number of owners, it is the biggest business of all by a considerable margin.

But what do we sell? Not "big" equipment. Not ten-ton trucks or bridge girders or even carload lots of nuts and bolts. We sell telephone service to individuals, and we sell it one call at a time. (We also provide networks of private communication lines for other business and for government, and long distance pathways interconnecting TV and radio stations. But these and other special services come to only 4 per cent of all our business.) The great bulk of our work is in handling one conversation after another, and most of these are local within the community calling area.

So, big as we are, at the same time we are a local retail business in each community. No distributor or middleman comes between us and our customers. We must live in the midst of each city or village we serve and know and heed the interests and wants of local people. We are a big business, in short, that must be a small business too in every home town we serve. When I say "be," I mean just that; this is not something that can be accomplished by make-believe.

What then are the values of our bigness? I think there are several and that each is important. Just as our need to be small in each community grows out of the nature of our service, so too does our need to be big.

A telephone is useless by itself. Its value is in reaching other people. The more telephones are interconnected, the greater the value. If everyone in town has phone service, that affords everyone more convenience than if half the people have it and half do not. And the value increases further when you can call anywhere you want—across the continent as well as across the street. So all the millions of telephone instruments, and the vast network of lines, and the thousands of switching offices, mean that we can give more value to each customer. In fact, this very size and abundance are really indispensable to a complete and fully satisfying service.

Moreover, all parts of the network must work well together. For all its size and sturdiness, a telephone system needs to be very precisely and delicately balanced. For instance, when you call Texas from Boston, many devices along the way continuously regulate the quality of the talking path—even compensating for differences in temperature. This is a simple illustration of how unified operation helps to achieve good service. And such service results not only from the co-ordination of equipment, but, more basically, from the co-ordination of human effort. Without both, good and dependable service would hardly be possible.

As I mentioned earlier, there are many other telephone companies which connect with the Bell System. It takes no credit from any of them to point out that a unifying, nationwide network increases the value of their service, just as their interconnection with us increases the value of ours. And to a marked degree the teamwork between Bell and non-Bell companies extends the co-ordination on which all good service depends. This I think only emphasizes further the inherent advantage of the Bell System's own setup.

Research and Technical Development

Telephone service is based on scientific discovery. It is the fruit of basic research that has brought much new knowledge and thousands of inventions. These inventions have then had to be organized into systems. All of this takes a massive co-ordinated research and development effort and requires a great deal of money. Without this large-scale effort, telephone progress as we have seen it could never have come about.

One man, Alexander Graham Bell, invented the telephone. This was one of the great inventions of all time. But it was a beginning, not an end, and Bell himself observed that to create a telephone *system* was the work of many minds. Today some fifteen thousand people, including more than forty-five hundred scientists and engineers, work in Bell Telephone Laboratories. Many in the group work on defense projects for the Government, but the main emphasis is on improving telephony.

Of course it is always an individual brain that makes a discovery. However, it is through the teamwork of many that we can best attack big problems and come up with the organized multitude of answers that are required. Very likely you have heard of the transistor. The basic transistor discoveries were made by three members of our Bell Laboratories. But they were made as part of a far-reaching effort to explore the nature of various solid materials and learn how they could be used to advance the art of communications. From this effort has come a whole new spectrum of developments which in the next generation will revolutionize telephony.

Research has already brought many big results in telephone service. It is this that has brought about long distance services;

local and long distance dialing systems; coaxial cable and radio relay systems that can carry TV programs as well as thousands of telephone conversations simultaneously over the same route.

It is this also that has enabled us to bring and keep the price of telephone service within the reach of millions. A telephone system is not like a water or electric power system, which can use the same line to serve additional customers. Whenever we serve a new customer, we must also provide additional facilities so that everyone else can reach him. So there is an inherent tendency for costs to go up as the telephone system grows. To combat this, Bell System research has continuously produced more efficient equipment, and our success in this respect goes to the very heart of telephone progress.

I conclude therefore that large-scale research by the Bell System is not merely an advantage. It is a necessity. And I might add here that keeping ahead in research also gives us opportunity to use the discoveries of others, in exchange for our giving them the right to use our inventions which are important to them. Clearly this too helps to keep the cost of telephone service down.

Perhaps it hardly needs to be said that projects big in design also have to be big in execution. A timely case in point is the development of transoceanic telephone cables.

The first of these was placed in service across the Atlantic in the autumn of 1956. Now there are several cables to Europe, with more planned; others to Alaska, Hawaii, Central and South America, the Caribbean area, and Bermuda; still others under construction westward from Hawaii across the Pacific.

These cables are a great step forward. They are free from atmospheric disturbances that sometimes trouble the radiotelephone, and talking over them is as easy as on any other call. This is the result of some thirty years or more of Bell Laboratories work in developing and testing reliable underwater "repeaters" which amplify the voice currents as much as a million times. But the cables are equally the product of heavy investment that now reaches into the hundreds of millions of dollars.

To give another example, we now have in operation, in cities across the country, long distance switching systems that automatically complete long distance calls dialed by telephone users. These systems likewise require investment in the hundreds of millions.

The meaning, I think, is clear. If we are to have the better, faster, and more convenient service that systems like these permit, we need organization on the scale that can plan and co-ordinate them; research on the scale that can bring them into being; and investment (with earnings to support it) on the scale that can pay for them and put them in the public service.

Manufacture and Supply

I have tried to indicate how co-ordination between the operating telephone companies benefits the service, and also how large-scale research brings about improvements and economies. A third function organized to the same ends is the manufacture and supply of telephone equipment. This is done by the Western Electric Company. By folding it in as part of the entire Bell System job, we get three-way teamwork. This to my mind is the key to success in serving the public.

All the experience of telephone operating people feeds back to research and manufacture. Everything in research goes out immediately to manufacturing and operations. Manufacture produces standard equipment of high quality that makes possible really effective co-ordination between the telephone companies. And manufacturing experience is enormously helpful to future research and design.

The important fact is that manufacture, like research, is embedded in the service organization. Western Electric people are just as devoted to the goal of giving service as their associates in the telephone companies. There is no dividing line, no divergence of interest, no motive at odds with the service motive. All work to the same end, and more closely than they could possibly do otherwise.

What is the practical result?

We continuously compare Western Electric equipment with that made by others, both as to quality and price. By every available test the equipment is superior and the price is less. No doubt Western's being the largest producer is an important factor in reducing its costs.

Western Electric earnings over the last ten years have averaged about 4 per cent of sales. That these earnings are moderate, to say the least, every other manufacturer well knows.

Western Electric never spares the horses to meet a Bell System need. Here are three illustrations:

1. In emergencies—fire, flood, hurricane, earthquake—telephone operating people know that Western will work around the clock to rush materials. (Incidentally, experience in disasters shows in several ways the value of a unified telephone organization. Repair forces from all points of the compass go to the disaster area. Western hurries along the supplies from strategically located distributing centers. Since the equipment and methods used by all companies of the System are the same, everybody is familiar with them and work proceeds quickly.)

2. Western produces in great volume what the Bell System needs in great volume. But the physical plant of the System is constantly changing. There are always small needs for replacement parts in equipment due to be changed in the future, but that in the meantime must be kept in perfect order. Western Electric has specially organized to meet these needs and makes thousands of items in small numbers, in addition to the things it makes in large numbers. This makes it possible to "evolutionize" the Bell System plant in the most efficient way.

3. With the end of World War II the public's demand for telephone service soared to unprecedented heights. Western Electric instantly took every risk involved in doubling its investment in production facilities in a few years' time. For another manufacturer to have taken comparable risks at the Bell System's request is inconceivable. But for Western Electric there was no question—because it is part of the telephone team, and service is the goal.

I might just add that Western Electric has been part of the Bell System since 1882. In those days, in the infancy of telephone service, manufacturers were turning out a vast confusion of telephone apparatus. There was a great need to set standards, and so the Bell organization bought Western and asked it to make equipment that would work at both ends, so to speak. In my own judgment, after having spent some thirty-seven years in the telephone companies and about three years as president of Western, I think this action, plus continuing research, has done more to give this country the best telephone service in the world than any other factor.

Defense Responsibilities

One other aspect of having a big and unified telephone organization needs mention. Communications are the first line of defense. The telephone system has a tremendous responsibility, which is shared by Bell and non-Bell companies alike. There is a great deal for all of us to do, and we work closely together to meet all military and civil defense needs. But I think everyone feels that the task is facilitated by the existence of a big organization through which a large share of the work can be co-ordinated.

As just one example, the Bell System has been building a great many so-called "express" telephone routes which bypass or go around centers that are potential targets for enemy attack. These we use for everyday service, but they are so planned that in event of disaster, emergency communications can be maintained. This is vital to the country, and it seems just as vital that there be a big organization that can work in close liaison with defense authorities and carry out plans of this sort. In fact, if the means for such co-ordination did not exist, I think they would have to be created.

Finally, the research and manufacturing skills of Bell Laboratories and Western Electric are of great value in designing and building communication and weapon systems for defense. We are asked to do a great deal of work on missile guidance systems. At the Atomic Energy Commission's request, we manage the Commission's Sandia Laboratory, which develops and designs atomic weapons. At the Air Force's request, we organized and carried out construction of the Distant Early Warning Line in the Arctic. We welcome these assignments when the Government says that our combination of skills, and the way we are organized, uniquely fit us for the task.

And when these assignments come to us, I reflect that if the Bell System setup has particular value for defense purposes, that also says quite a lot about its value for regular telephone service purposes. For the fact is that many military problems today, involving the development and operation of complex systems, are rather like the telephone problems we are dealing with all the time. So I conclude that if it is important from the military standpoint that there be such an organization as ours, it is equally important that the same combination continue to do its best toward the purpose for which it was originally intended—namely, to give the public an ever improving telephone service.

Service and Profits

A few months ago someone asked me, "Which do you put first in your mind, service or profits?" When I said that naturally I put service first, he seemed a little surprised. This puzzled me until I reflected that for years after World War II, the telephone companies repeatedly had to ask the regulatory commissions for increased rates; and with that in mind, my questioner had perhaps decided that our first interest is in money.

This cannot be. The function of the Bell System must be to serve the public and serve it well. But we can only serve by earning money—and enough to keep ourselves in good financial shape so that we can go ahead with research and keep on making service improvements.

The whole matter can be put in two very short sentences. They are: We must serve well to prosper. We must prosper to serve well.

This may sound elementary. And the reasons why the Bell companies have had to increase rates are elementary also. We have been plagued by inflation, just like everyone else. Our costs have gone up and are still rising. Wage increases alone have more than equaled all the increases in Bell telephone rates since before the war.

What is not so elementary is the question, "Just how much

should a telephone company earn?" I am going to state my view in a way that may not have occurred to some. I think we should earn enough so that in the long run the cost of service to telephone users will be *lower* than if we earned *less.*

At first this may seem a bit of a paradox. But is it? Just consider: Only with good earnings can we conduct the business most efficiently. Only with ample resources can we push research in such a way that we will get better and more efficient equipment at the earliest possible moment. Only if we have enough money can we spend money in ways that will reduce the cost of service in the long run.

For instance, think of any community whose telephone needs are growing. A new central office that will meet those needs for a reasonable period ahead will cost more at the start than a smaller office that will only meet them for a very short time. But the smaller office will then have to be enlarged, and this will cost more in the end. If we are so scrimped from year to year that we have to build piecemeal, this is bound to increase the cost of service in the long run. But if we are financially able and free to do the right kind of job at the start, the average cost through the years will be less.

Under present conditions, I believe that earnings in the neighborhood of 8 per cent on the capital invested in the Bell System will give the best long-run assurance of excellent service at the lowest possible price. Such a return, incidentally, compares with average postwar earnings of more than 12 per cent by large manufacturing companies, with which the Bell System must compete for new capital.

Regulation

Eight per cent is more than the Bell System earns today and more than a good many regulatory commissions have been willing to allow. And some commissions have limited earnings quite severely. If the principle I have set forth above is correct, why is this so?

No doubt it is partly because many regulatory people have yet to be convinced that the thesis is sound. For many years the habit of regulation has been more to apply restrictions than to take them away. There has grown up quite a body of belief that the way to keep rates low is to keep earnings low—even though this particular pudding has no proof. To depart from this dogma (I almost want to call it folklore) is not easy. To do it the commissions must not only be convinced that the right course is to regulate up rather than down. They must also have the very considerable courage that is needed to take the political responsibility.

Yet I am sure that just such courage is needed to give this country the best and most economical service in years to come. We in the Bell System have studied this matter carefully. We know that electric and gas utilities that earn relatively well give as good or better service—*at lower rates* on the average—than those that earn poorly. We know our own Bell telephone rates are lower on the average in states where earnings are better than average. I don't cite these examples as scientific proof, but they do suggest the possibilities in a little less restriction, a little more freedom.

There is no law I know of that prevents reasonable freedom under regulation. There is none that requires regulation to be timid or slow, or to put its reliance in technicalities. And I want to say that the Bell System is in no way opposed to regulation. We are not merely not opposed to it, we are for it—and this is no lip service. A business like ours, which doesn't have competition in the same degree as many others, has to be regulated. But this doesn't make us different from other people. We react to incentives and opportunity just as they do. We too need good earnings and ample resources to put in improvements and economies. We too need freedom—under regulation—to do our very best.

The Human Effort to Serve

Clearly telephone employees must be considerate of the needs and wishes of telephone users. This is the essence of good service, and is doubly important because our customers cannot go elsewhere if we should fail them. But good and considerate service can only be rendered by people who sincerely want to meet the needs of others. To feel that way about their jobs, they must also feel that their own needs are being considered.

Will the telephone installer, for example, do his courteous best to help a family make sure their telephones are installed in the most convenient locations?

That depends partly on his nature and his training. But it also depends on whether he thinks he is fairly treated by his boss; on the general atmosphere he works in; and on whether he trusts his company to do the right thing by him according to his abilities. Underlying all these must be the understanding that every employee is important as an individual and needs a work environment which gives opportunities for personal growth.

The same factors also influence the installer's boss, and so on all along the line. And it is the sum of the attitudes of everyone in the business, along with their abilities, that determines how well the Bell System will serve the nation.

Let me list briefly some of the things we think are most important to the success of our human effort.

Wages and Opportunity

First is to pay good wages. We need able people and should pay them accordingly. On the other hand, to pay more than similar abilities command elsewhere in the community would seem to give telephone people a special privilege at our customers' expense. We think therefore that we ought to keep telephone wages well up in the "good pay" range, but not out in front of everybody else.

Second, employees want the chance to get ahead. This is essential to a good working climate and getting a good job done. So we must not only provide opportunity, but also help people prepare themselves for it.

On the side of providing opportunity there are several practical needs, in addition to the basic requirement of keeping the business progressive and financially healthy. For example, there has to be a just and orderly plan for the retirement of older people. The Bell companies have had pension retirement plans (paid for entirely by the companies) since 1913, with pensions directly related to wages and years of service. Today the social importance of pension systems is generally recognized, but I want to point out again that in a business like ours, having an orderly retirement procedure makes a tremendous contribution to good service, for it keeps the way open for promotion and continually provides incentives to younger people.

Another big factor in providing opportunity is to spread authority as much as possible. Maybe some people still have the idea that a few top managers in a big business run the whole show, and everyone else does what he is told. The truth is we couldn't conduct the Bell System that way even if we wanted to, and we don't want to. That kind of management couldn't begin to produce a good telephone service. As I said earlier, good service begins in each local community, and it is simply impossible for faraway higher-ups to know all the whys and wherefores of local needs and act effectively to meet them. Responsibility and authority *must* be decentralized, and the more the better.

Decentralizing not only provides opportunity, but helps people prepare themselves for more of it. I think it is well known that the Bell System is an up-from-the-ranks business. No large share-owning interest dominates the management or says who the top managers shall be. They have to come up the ladder step by step. So it is vitally important that we push out responsibility and authority as much as we can, and give able people the kind of training that comes from having to make decisions and live with them.

Training

This is not a matter of pushing people off the dock to see if they can swim. To help men and women prepare themselves for opportunity, we must train them in specific skills. We must also, I feel sure, tell them freely and frankly about the progress of the business, answer their questions without quibbling, and generally do everything we can to bring about good communications and understanding up and down the line of organization.

Beyond this, we see a real need for, and are widely using, organized study, conference, and discussion. These programs are aimed at helping members of management to grow in skill and stature *as managers;* to test their thinking when confronted by other points of view; to chew on tough problems of the sort they might have to face in new job assignments; to see their immediate jobs in relation to the success of the whole business; and to broaden their understanding of social and economic forces and the place of the Bell System in the world we are trying to serve.

Good pay plus opportunity for personal growth, and with these, decentralized authority and a continuing effort to help people increase in understanding as well as in skill—these to me are some of the essential factors in the Bell System's human effort. No more than any other group of people are we free from human shortcomings. But I think these things I have been discussing have been helpful to a good telephone job in the past, and of course what we want is that they should be even more so in the future.

Self-Examination

I get quite a few letters from telephone users. Many express appreciation for good service, and these give a lift to all concerned. A larger proportion are critical of some service incident or situation. Sometimes this is due to misunderstanding, but that only means we have failed to bring understanding about. In every case we need to do the most we can to correct the fault.

I think there is wide agreement that this country has the best telephone service in the world. With 6 per cent of the world's population we have about half of all the world's telephones, and travelers coming back from abroad usually say that for courtesy, speed, dependability, and ease of calling anywhere, our service is out in front.

However there is a tremendous amount still to be done, and that is the thought I want to emphasize. We telephone people need to look at ourselves even more critically than anyone else might.

As a starter, we don't rely on letters to the chairman to find out what the public thinks and wants. In addition to making our own continuous measurements of every phase of performance, we try to write down and analyze *all* criticisms and comments. We also go out and interview people to learn their attitudes and preferences. Many times, in order to ascertain a community's wishes, we have visited every customer in town.

As a result of these activities, thousands of Bell System practices have been changed through the years. This is a continuous process. But there are also times when there is no practical way to do exactly what a customer might like—at least right at the moment. This may be because the technical means do not yet exist, or because the cost is prohibitive, or because meeting the wishes of one person might do injury to another, and so on. In such cases I think we have the greatest possible obligation to give good reasons as reasonable people, and not to be arbitrary.

But there is an even worse way to be arbitrary than not to give reasonable explanations. This is to be arbitrary by inertia, so to speak—I mean, to be generally satisfied with things as they are.

A Progressive Spirit

If a business isn't progressive and forward looking, it doesn't take the public long to find that out. This is as true for us as for any other business. While we may not compete in quite the same way retail stores do, or makers of shoes or sealing-wax, we don't lack spurs to a better job. We compete with other forms of communications, and with transport systems, and also with all other industry for our share of what the public has available to spend. This means too that we need to promote and sell. There is simply no basis for the old saw that "everybody has a phone, so you don't need to advertise." One of the main reasons for the growth of telephone service is the fact that we have promoted and sold it. Moreover this is indispensable to a vigorous and progressive spirit among employees. They compete with each other and the various Bell companies likewise compete with each other in every phase of the job.

I deeply believe that Americans have gained a great deal from the development of telephone service in the American way, as a free private enterprise under public regulation. It can be stated as a fact that most of the great advances in telephony have been made in this country. And they have been made rapidly. Few people today recall that when World War I began, it was not even possible to telephone across the United States. Today it is a matter of a minute or so (and more and more frequently, only a few seconds); the cost is about one-tenth of what it used to be; and during evening and night hours the cost is even less than that. Moreover the average cost of all telephone service (notwithstanding the increases in price since the end of World War II) is a smaller part of most household budgets than it was in the past. Twenty-five years ago it took three and a half hours' work each month for the average factory worker to earn enough to have a telephone in his home. Today it takes him two and a quarter hours. Incidentally, this makes telephone rates in this country the cheapest in the world, in relation to consumer income.

In the Future, More for More People

I am confident that given reasonable freedom and good earnings, the telephone companies in years to come will be able to do even more in the public interest. In the last fifteen years our technical progress has been greater than ever before. Already millions of people can dial long distance calls directly, in a few seconds' time. By 1965 this will be the general practice for most everyone. As a practical matter, the difference between local and long distance service is beginning to disappear.

In the research laboratories, entirely new all-electronic switching systems are now under development. The first electronic exchange will be opened in 1965 and others will follow rapidly. In the years to come, these will make possible many new and useful services. Likewise, new methods will be available for transmitting all kinds of information, including person-to-person television.

Progress of this sort gives people an increasing range of choice in communication service. Today this can be illustrated by the variety of telephone instruments and the many ways they can be arranged to suit personal convenience. For instance, we can offer telephones specially suited for kitchen or bedroom, various telephone systems for different office layouts, speakerphones that may be used without lifting the receiver, telephones particularly designed for noisy locations, and so on. And systems for the transmission of data are growing fast in versatility and use.

Here it may seem that I am getting down to details. But the idea behind all this is far from being a detail. People may (and frequently do) think of the telephone company as a monopoly. In the sense that we don't compete with other telephone companies in the same area, that is true. The public long ago decided that to have two companies competing in that fashion would be wasteful. But that still gives us no license for what you might call monopolistic behavior. Our license is simply to give the best possible service, and we think that definitely means giving our customers every practical option or choice to get what they want. This is the real drive behind the kind of thing I have been sketching out here.

At the same time, I want to say strongly that the Bell System does not intend to step outside its proper sphere of providing communications that serve the public interest. We have no wish to grow bigger merely for the sake of aggrandizement. Our job rather is to make our bigness—this vast network of lines and instruments and switching systems, which has no counterpart anywhere else in the world—to make this abundance more freely and easily useful to everyone; so that we can say to each telephone user in each community, "All this is at your service—and there will be more."

From Talks at
A. T. & T. Share Owners' Annual Meetings

FROM TALKS AT A. T. & T. SHARE OWNERS' ANNUAL MEETINGS

1957

Construction

I think most of the share owners understand that to meet the public's needs for good service we have to go ahead and install the equipment required to provide it. But every so often one of you writes to me and asks if we really need to spend so much.

We neither want nor intend to raise or spend one unnecessary dollar. If other businesses are deciding to spend less than they had planned some months ago, I assume this is because their studies tell them that's the right thing for them to do. But we must face the facts of *our* business.

Our construction budget is built up step by step on the basis of the most careful analyses and estimates we know how to make, and is under constant review. It isn't big because we want it to be big. It's big because the country's need for service requires it to be big.

Remember that the population of this country is increasing by nearly three million people a year. New households are forming all the time and most of them need and want telephone service. You might put it this way—that each month our basic market increases to an extent roughly equal to a new city the size of Worcester, Massachusetts, or Tulsa, Oklahoma.

We must also keep ahead of the ever growing need for long distance service. Last year our long distance business was up nearly 10 per cent. But assume that in the long run the average increase may be considerably less; even so, the construction job is tremendous. For example, an increase of only 6 per cent a year would mean a total increase of 50 per cent over today's volume in seven years. We have learned by experience that we must build ahead of that kind of growth or suffer poor service.

We also have a great deal of construction to keep on top of the government's needs for defense communications. This is an absolute must. Fully adequate communications are vital to the country's security, and we cannot fall short of meeting our responsibility.

We must provide the services people expect and are entitled to receive. The whole welfare of the business is wrapped up in this undertaking.

Earnings

Every cent we obtain from investors and use to build the telephone plant must, of course, be earned on. I'd like to bring out several aspects of the effort the Bell companies are making to maintain and increase the earnings on your investment.

The first necessity in these days of creeping inflation is to keep ahead of rising costs. We do everything we can to hold costs down. We develop and install more efficient equipment. We devise new tools. We are continuously working out more economical methods for handling all the many different jobs that go into the rendering of telephone service. But in spite of these savings, our costs, in which wages are much the largest element, continue to go up.

So this is one factor in our requests to the regulatory commissions for rate increases: we must have higher revenues to cover higher costs.

A second factor is equally important. This is the need to assure successful financing on a scale never before attempted by any business.

To meet the public's wants we must obtain great sums of money from investors—more new capital than ever before. We must do this at a time when money is tight and interest rates are high; and in doing it we must win and keep the favor of investors in competition with all industry, including nonregulated companies which earn two or three or more times as much on their investment as we have been able to earn under public regulation. This clearly means that the Bell System, in order to have reasonable assurance of attracting all the capital it needs, should have earnings substantially above the present level.

There's one other aspect of this subject of earnings that I'd like to discuss, so that you may further understand the point of view that telephone people bring to their dealings with the commissions. This is the fundamental conception that ample profits will produce better goods and services than lean profits—and produce them at less cost to the consumer.

There's nothing mysterious about this. It's only common sense. You know from everyday experience that financially successful businesses put better values on the shelf for you to choose from. That's because they can afford to improve their operations and develop new and better products at reasonable prices. This is what you get when a business is earning well enough to manage for the long pull.

Our business is no different. Good profits provide both the incentive and the means toward a better job and greater value. But if earnings are low, and all energies and judgment must be directed to meet the pressing needs of the moment, it becomes impossible to do the best for the long run.

I'll give a practical illustration. Here's a telephone engineer who is figuring out what size telephone cable should be installed to serve a growing neighborhood. He knows it must serve two hundred homes right away. He's reasonably sure also that in another couple of years perhaps two hundred more homes will want service. Putting in a cable today that is big enough to serve all four hundred homes will cost more *at the start.* However, putting in a smaller cable today that will serve only two hundred, and another of equal size two years from now, *will cost a lot more in the end.*

What will the engineer do?

If the company is pinched for money, he'll have to put in the smaller cable today, even though this will be more expensive in the long run. But if the company is in good financial shape—if it can readily get the capital required for the big cable—and if the general level of earnings justifies absorbing the temporarily higher cost of the larger cable, until the time when its full capacity is utilized—then the engineer will decide to go ahead with that. Over the years this will save money and produce more economical service. It's a good long-pull investment that benefits telephone users.

Now, telephone people are called on to make thousands of decisions like this all the time, day in and day out; and the fact is that in all these decisions, reasonable prosperity is essential to assure the most economy and progress.

This is just as true in our business as in any other. We operate under regulation because we don't have direct competition to the same degree that many other businesses have it. This is right and proper and as it should be. But it doesn't mean that the principles of progress for us are one bit different from the principles of progress for others. And in the framework of regulation, the commissions have full freedom to approve rates and earnings that will stimulate progress, increase incentives, nourish innovation—and in the long run, as I have said, bring telephone users the greatest value.

There is a sort of popular formula that low earnings mean low rates and good earnings mean high rates.

All I can say is that this is a misconception, and a most unfortunate one. The truth is that regulated utilities which earn relatively well give as good or better service at lower rates than those which earn relatively poorly. I assure you this is not wishful thinking; it can be demonstrated and we are taking every opportunity to do so.

The commissions have a responsibility that calls for much wisdom and foresight. Also, authorizing good earnings sometimes calls for a high degree of political courage. Such action, however, in the long run will return the greatest value to the public, and the commissions themselves will surely find more satisfaction in that result than in any other.

Fortunately, from the standpoint of the individual telephone user our rate needs are small. They usually come to not more than a few cents a day on the average customer's bill. Nevertheless these few pennies a day are vitally important to assure that the American people will continue to have the best communication service in the world. With this need made clear, I have full faith that the public will approve constructive and forward-looking action by the commissions.

1958

Improvements in Methods

Management effort to bring about a better job has been going on for a great many years and I am sure it always will. To give one broad measure of the result, in the last thirty years the number of Bell System telephones has increased four times, from about thirteen million to more than fifty-two million. In the same period the number of people who provide the service has more than doubled.

What has made this possible? The answer is: We have better equipment. We are always developing better tools. We try constantly to improve our operating methods. These reflect management leadership—effective research—careful training—and the exercise of American ingenuity by countless telephone men and women. All these together have made telephone service faster, more convenient, and more valuable. At the same time they have made our human effort less tiresome, less toilsome, and much better organized. It is this combination of more attractive service and better methods of providing service that brings us more customers, earns dividends for our share owners, and provides opportunity for telephone employees.

Sales Effort

Another range of activity that is vital to an efficient and resultful telephone job is the vigorous merchandising, promotion, and sale of service.

Telephone people sell service in many ways. They sell it with the help of advertising. They sell it when customers visit our business offices. They sell it over the telephone. They sell it when they visit homes to install and maintain telephone instruments.

They sell it by studying the usage of service by business firms, and then showing how modernized telephone arrangements can increase their efficiency and help to bring in more business for them.

They sell it by demonstrating to businessmen that they can profitably use long distance service to get new orders—to keep in touch with their customers—and to thank buyers for orders.

They sell it by finding new and profitable locations for public telephones.

In all this work, I assure you we are aiming straight at the goal of getting the most return on your investment, while at the same time providing the best service for the customer.

For example, it is better from every standpoint to install complete home service all at once than it is to put in one telephone on the first visit, and then later another, and still later another.

It is better from the user's standpoint for at least two reasons. First, he or she gets the most complete and convenient service right away. Second, there is less to pay in service connection charges.

It is better from our standpoint, also, because the revenue is larger from the start, and one visit by the telephone installer costs the company much less than three visits. Last year 55 per cent of all the additional home telephones we installed went in at the same time that we first installed service, and we certainly hope to improve this performance as we go along.

Toward the Best Possible Service

In Western Electric manufacturing, last year there were more than a thousand projects afoot to reduce the costs of production. Likewise, in the telephone companies we have hundreds of undertakings always going on to improve our methods of building and operating telephone facilities and promoting and selling our service.

All these projects are in close association with the continuous research and development work of Bell Telephone Laboratories. Technical advances open up the road to progress, and then we go on from there. Research, manufacture, and operations all proceed together, and all have a common goal. This is to provide the best possible service to customers, and at the same time earn a satisfactory profit.

This last point is vital, and I emphasize particularly that we have it always in mind. We are fully aware, also, that to produce good earnings, nothing can take the place of adequate telephone rates. Our efforts to improve equipment and methods have been very resultful. They have helped a great deal to keep our costs down. Nevertheless, by themselves they could not possibly overcome the steep inflation of the last twenty years.

So our full job as we see it is to keep improving service—to keep chipping away at costs—to promote and sell effectively—and along with these things, to unfailingly present our needs to the regulatory commissions wherever the rates for service are not what they should be. Certainly we don't enjoy increasing telephone rates—but if, in the long run, inflation continues to increase our costs, I see no alternative.

This makes it all the more important, of course, to push steadily ahead along the lines I have illustrated today. To earn the money we need, we must surely give telephone users the best and most valuable service we know how to provide. That is the necessary basis—the only possible basis—for obtaining the rates that will produce good earnings on your investment. I have every confidence that we shall continue to be successful in this, and on behalf of your Board of Directors and all in Bell System management, I want to say to every share owner that you can count on us to do our utmost in your behalf.

1959

A Long-Run View

We are in good shape and have good prospects ahead. In this growing country, the services we provide are more and more wanted and more and more used; at the same time, we are continuing to improve existing services and develop new ones, and we are making our operations more efficient. All these factors hold great promise for the future.

We have also done a vast amount of work to make our communication system a strong bulwark of defense. As the annual report pointed out, we have a growing network of alternate routes that go around critical areas, and we are building our whole system bigger—stronger—more flexible—as every day goes by.

To mention now the proposed stock split, I should like to say again, as we have in previously published statements, that in recommending a split your Board of Directors had no thought of changing the essential character of this business. We have never favored an up-and-down dividend policy and we are no more disposed to that now than we ever were. Our responsibility as we see it is to do the best long-run job we can for every share owner, both small and large, just as in providing service we are responsible to every customer. We shall continue to act on that principle and there will be no departure from it.

Research and Development

This afternoon I will talk a little about our effort to discover, develop, and introduce new devices and systems that will provide better service and do it more economically than the devices and systems which step by step they supersede. If it were not for this technical progress, our costs today would be far higher and our need for rate increases far greater.

Or to look at the matter from a different angle:

What inflation does is eat up the dollar savings that come from technical gains. I'm going to discuss, for instance, some of the steps involved in introducing what we call Direct Distance Dialing, or DDD. As I go along, you may reflect that this represents a vast economic gain as well as a service improvement. If it were not for inflation, I'm sure in my own mind that this kind of progress would take us far along the road to lower prices, better earnings—in fact, better everything for everyone. But inflation erases the economic gain and thereby puts a penalty on us all.

This is all I shall say on that score, but I hope that in your thinking on the subject, this is a fact that you will not overlook.

One other introductory comment. We have often emphasized the importance of three-way teamwork between the research, manufacturing, and operating organizations in the Bell System. As a matter of fact this teamwork has never been better than during the past year and I am happy here to pay tribute to the work that has been done by all the men and women concerned. I am sure the share owners generally appreciate the need for research—using that word broadly to include both basic research and technical development. I'm less certain that the value—in fact the necessity—for intimate teamwork between research, manufacturing, and operating people is fully understood.

To turn now to the example I mentioned, let us consider the development of Direct Distance Dialing, or DDD.

The story begins where you would naturally expect—in the desire of the telephone companies to provide faster, more attractive, more efficient service. Year by year and place by place, they have been extending dial service to handle *local* calls. And the most modern of these dial systems—the so-called crossbar system developed at Bell Laboratories—offered great opportunities to develop *nationwide* dialing.

First came years of study by telephone engineers to set up a basic plan for interconnecting all parts of the country. They knew of course how different dial exchanges in big cities were being interconnected so that our customers could dial local calls directly. Distance dialing, as they visualized it, would be a vast extension of this principle.

A transitional step (starting about fifteen years ago) was dialing by operators. The caller gives the operator the number—and she dials straight through to the distant telephone. No operator is needed at the distant end.

In planning all such changes, our telephone engineers work not only with each other—they also work constantly with the people at Bell Telephone Laboratories who design dial equipment. Thus Direct Distance Dialing is their common concern. Moreover, both the telephone engineers and the Laboratories men are working closely with the people of Western Electric who will build, deliver, and install the apparatus needed.

This intimate co-operation takes many forms. There is time to indicate only a few.

At the Laboratories, for instance, engineers conceived a new form of fast-moving switch that they believed could be very useful in DDD.

But one vital question was—could it be made at low enough cost? So while the men at the Laboratories worked on the design, they asked Western Electric engineers to work with them on a method for manufacturing the switch in quantity. This joint effort produced a remarkable machine which automatically assembles 360 switches an hour, at a cost of a few cents apiece. Each is designed and built to work reliably for at least forty years.

Three-Way Teamwork

And I call your attention to this: Western Electric threw its energy and skill into the job right along with the telephone companies and the Laboratories to help reach the common goal. Only this unified, three-way teamwork makes it possible to introduce service improvements with greatest efficiency and economy.

As another illustration, let us consider some of the things that took place when long distance dialing equipment was installed in Wilmington, Delaware.

This was placed in service on March 15—just a month ago. But three years before was when the project began, with several co-ordinating groups working on the job.

The fact is, it was not only in Wilmington that we were doing our work, but in many other places that had to be connected into the new system. All told, there were fifty-seven cities and towns where equipment was installed and made ready for interconnection—and every bit of it on a precise schedule pointing toward service on March 15, 1959.

In some of these fifty-seven places one kind of apparatus had to be adjusted or modified to work with the new system—in other places, another kind—and changes were necessary not only inside the telephone exchanges but on the outside lines as well.

To facilitate such work, Western Electric keeps full records of nearly every Bell System telephone office. These show the exact location of every piece of equipment in thousands of local exchanges and show also where every wire terminates.

Information in this form is tremendously valuable in times of disaster or emergency; it helps start the wheels rolling instantly to produce and supply everything needed to restore service. However it is also extremely useful in normal times as well as in emergencies. In the case of this DDD project, it speeds up the work of specifying exactly what new equipment is needed in each place. And from this we go right on to the orderly scheduling of manufacture, to the shipment and installation of apparatus, and to the training of people who will operate and maintain it.

These then are some of the co-operative steps that bring about the extension of Direct Distance Dialing. But this system we are bringing into use is made up of many, many parts. Let me indicate briefly how some of the parts came into existence.

For instance, with DDD we have *automatic alternate routing*. That is, when you dial your call, if all lines are busy on the route that is normally used, in a fraction of a second the equipment automatically picks out another line on another route.

Of course this did not just happen. Years ago the telephone operating engineers asked—can we give faster, more economical service by selecting alternate routes automatically? And again they considered the problem jointly with the Laboratories—and the Laboratories went ahead to devise apparatus that would do the job.

This apparatus we call a card translator. One of the interesting things about card translators is that they use transistors. In fact this was the first use of transistors in the telephone system.

Basic Research

Now the transistor, of course, resulted from basic research at our Laboratories. And research in many fields lies behind the development and design of DDD: research in metallurgy and chemistry, for instance, to develop the various alloys and other materials used; mathematical studies of the problems the equipment must deal with; and physical research in the behavior of solid materials—what the scientists call "solid state physics." Out of this came development of transistors and many related devices which will be used in entirely new electronic switching systems now being designed in the laboratory.

The point is that with a well-rounded, unified research organization—a balanced scientific community, so to speak—our teamwork goes the whole distance from the daily rendering of service, all the way back to the work of scientists who are asking questions of nature.

Here is still another aspect of the story: Our switching equipment wouldn't be worth anything if we didn't have plenty of pathways to switch *to*. We need tremendous numbers of lines between cities. And the process of bringing them into use—from research to development to manufacture to service—needs the same kind of co-operation that we have already seen.

Years ago Bell Laboratories pioneered electronic methods for sending many long distance messages simultaneously over one pair of wires. Then came the Laboratories' development of coaxial cable systems, which handle great numbers of conversations over a hollow tube with a single wire inside it. Next came radio relay systems, which like coaxial cables can also carry thousands of conversations, and television. These use new kinds of apparatus to transmit, receive, and amplify radio signals which vibrate billions of times a second.

Working Together

To get these new systems into production—to make them available in time to handle the tremendous increase in long distance calling in the postwar years—to be prepared to carry television programs across the country—called for a degree of cooperation which would have been impossible if operations, research, and manufacture had not been teamed together.

Again, in telephone cable design and manufacture, Bell Laboratories men work in Western Electric plants side by side with the manufacturing engineers. Out of their work in recent years have come new and better cables to meet the telephone companies' needs. All cables used to require an outer covering of lead. Now we have new coverings that are equally sturdy and moisture-proof, but are less costly, lighter in weight, and quite a bit easier to handle.

For years also the wires in cables were insulated with paper or a coating of paper pulp. Now we have developed a new cable with plastic-insulated wires. This is manufactured at Western Electric's new Omaha plant by new and pioneering methods. It is the finest cable ever made, and it will permit further economies in telephone operation.

We are making similar joint progress in many other fields. Telephone people test out new kinds of instruments in homes and offices. While the tests are being made, operating engineers work hand in hand with the instrument designers and the production men—pooling their efforts to meet problems of design, manufacture, and marketing.

At Western's plant in the Merrimack Valley, similar teamwork is creating apparatus to make our local telephone wires work more efficiently. We have new equipment, for example, that can be used economically to multiply voice pathways on a single pair of wires *even over short distances.* And a brand-new transistorized amplifier makes it possible to use thinner wires to interconnect local exchanges inside the same metropolitan area. In other words, we are now making improvements and economies in systems of the same general kind that we have used for years on the long distance network, so that we can begin to use them effectively in local telephone systems.

At still another Western Electric plant—in Allentown—we are working to solve the various problems involved in manufacturing transistors. Here our engineering teams design not only the transistors themselves, but also the machines needed to produce them in quantity. Work on a machine that automatically assembles one kind of transistor began in 1951, long before anyone had much idea what form the transistor itself might take. Such overlapping has been invaluable in getting ready for big-volume production of transistors which will be used in new electronic telephone switching systems.

Quality and Compatibility

I shall sum up with a few main points:

First, it is vital to the service we provide—and equally vital to our financial success—that we design, build, and operate equipment of the very highest quality; equipment just as dependable and reliable as we know how to make.

Second, all the trillions of parts in the telephone system must work well together. We must design and build our facilities to suit local needs in each community—but also, every part in each town and city must be in harmony with all the rest. Many types of equipment have been built into the ever changing network at different times over many years. Each type must be kept compatible with every other type at all times.

Now these fundamentals—top quality and dependability—plus complete compatibility between all parts—are basic operating needs. It is therefore essential that research and development people and manufacturing people, as well as the operating people themselves, think first, last, and all the time of how to reach operating goals.

In our three-way organization, all telephone operating experience guides research, development, and manufacture. Everything in research and development flows directly to manufacturing and operations. Manufacture produces top quality equipment for operations, and manufacturing experience is enormously helpful to future development and design.

This close co-ordination gives dynamic drive to the business; and the proof of the pudding is that under this form of organization we have pioneered most of the major advances in the art of telephony, and from the beginning have provided America with the most and the best telephone service in the world.

1960

Dividend Policy

At last year's meeting I discussed the Company's dividend policy in terms that may bear repeating. I said, "We have never favored an up-and-down dividend policy and we are no more disposed to that now than we have ever been. Our responsibility as we see it is to do the best long-run job we can for every share owner, just as in providing service we are responsible to every customer."

This means among other things that we do not believe our dividends should be paid according to any formula that would relate current payout to current earnings—for in such case, up-and-down variations in earnings would call for corresponding up-and-down change in the dividend. Historically there have been no reductions in A. T. & T. dividends, and none of us wants to think of lowering a dividend rate once it has been established. This is basic in the character of the business.

To me this simply emphasizes further the importance of not making premature decisions. When we proceed on the basis that what goes up ought not to come down, then the decisions we make must rest on a foundation of solid experience, careful consideration of all factors that may affect the future, and reasonable assurance that whatever action is ultimately taken, we shall be able to stay with it for the long pull.

Financing

As in past years, we shall continue to need large amounts of new capital to finance our construction. During the last five years the Bell System's new capital requirements have averaged well over a billion dollars a year, and in the years ahead I doubt that they will average anything less.

We cannot forecast what form our future financing may take. Those of you who have held shares for some years know that from time to time we have used various different methods to raise money. Looking ahead, I can only say that we shall consider all available means, and at any given time choose the method that we believe will best serve the needs of the business and the long-run interests of the share owners. One consideration in our thinking has always been to keep the proportion of debt in total capital, whenever possible, somewhere broadly in the range between 30 and 40 per cent. This objective will continue to guide us. However, whether a particular step in our financing program will take the form of bonds, convertible debentures, or stock must depend on other factors as well.

All this emphasizes again how fast this business of ours is growing. But I think that even more important than the fact of growth is the *manner* in which we grow. In my judgment we must grow as a progressive business that can constantly do more for more people. We must grow as a business that is regarded as alert, efficient, and always up to date. We must grow as a business that knows how to make improvements in service pay. We must grow as a business that can meet competition wherever it may develop. We must grow as a business in which ideals of service and marketing talent and zest for discovery all meet and mingle and strengthen each other.

Space Communications

The telephone was invented eighty-four years ago last month. Ever since then Bell System research has led the way in making possible fast, convenient, dependable, low-cost communication services—throughout local communities, throughout the nation, across the oceans, and around the world. We have discovered a vast amount of new knowledge and we have kept in the forefront of all knowledge that can contribute to our job. We have kept out in front—we are determined to stay out in front—and we are just as determined to lead the field in space communications.

We already know a lot about the problems and possibilities. Our scientists at Bell Laboratories have developed new types of equipment that hold great promise. They are currently engaged with the National Aeronautics and Space Administration in a series of experiments that will test out the possibilities for worldwide communication via one form of space satellite. They have other concepts very much in mind. And they know how to guide satellites into orbit, too; in fact the Tiros satellite, the one that has been taking pictures of the cloud cover of the earth, was guided into the most nearly circular orbit ever achieved, by a system developed and designed at Bell Laboratories and produced by Western Electric. This is the same guidance system that has been so successful in guiding the Titan intercontinental ballistic missile. It is extremely versatile and I have been informed that it will be used in the future to guide numerous space vehicles.

This is not the time or the place for predictions, and I shall make none. But I do want to make clear to the share owners, and with utmost emphasis, that the Bell System is right now at the forefront of knowledge in space communications, and that is where we intend to stay.

While space may well widen the future areas of competition in our business, we are no less alert to the fact that there is already plenty of competition close to the ground. This is why I emphasized a moment ago that we must grow as a business that can meet competition wherever it may develop. I am confident we shall do this. We have technical know-how in great abundance, as I have said. We have a nationwide network that is absolutely unmatched, and we are constantly learning how to use it in new ways that offer great advantages to present and future customers. We have an organization of people who have abilities and spirit second to none.

Freedom to Manage

With all these, the continuing essential is that we have real freedom to manage. This is necessary to good performance in any business, and ours is no exception. Good earnings, and good profits, for instance, are fundamental to our ability to make the investments in the future that produce progress. Regulation, necessary as it may be, must still leave room for adequate incentives and adequate rewards. And the general attitude of government must be such as will encourage effort, rather than discourage it. We deeply want to be—and our country *needs* us to be—a vital, buoyant, dynamic force for progress. To be this kind of force, this kind of organization, this kind of people, we need reasonable freedom; freedom under regulation, to be sure, but freedom just the same.

1961

Construction and Earnings

Our construction program as you know is very large, around two and a half billion dollars—in fact this is why we need to finance on such a big scale. However we have planned our construction carefully, not only to take care of growth but also to invest in improvements that stimulate new uses of our network and increase operating efficiency.

Organizing our program in this way, at a time when the pace of growth is not so feverish as it has been at other times, has very practical advantages. It prepares us to do more for our customers in the months and years ahead. It strengthens our long-run capacity to earn. It keeps employment up—both employment within the business and also in industries that provide us with goods and services. Furthermore, some of the work we are doing will further increase our ability to meet possible defense emergencies. An important example is the construction of a new deep-buried long distance cable system, with amplifier stations along the route all underground, as well as the cable itself. We are also preparing to lay certain new ocean cables a bit ahead of immediate business needs, but consistent with foreseeable international and military requirements for service.

We expect to maintain earnings levels that will appropriately support our financing. Today as always, however, we depend on both federal and state regulatory bodies' seeing the wisdom of earnings that will keep the Bell System in good financial health and assure first-rate service at reasonable cost. In recent years we have been able to improve both service and earnings by introducing better equipment, widening our service offerings, and increasing efficiency. When these efforts are effective, as they have been, we do not believe that regulators should penalize progress and destroy incentives by putting a low ceiling on profits. As long as profits are within a reasonable range—and there is no part of the Bell System today where they are above that—we need the leeway that spurs effort and brings about real progress.

A good example is interstate long distance service. Earnings on this part of our business are better today than a few years ago, and at the same time the users are getting better service at no increase in price. Looking back a bit further, interstate telephone rates are now lower than they were before the war, and at today's volume of business the public is paying a billion dollars a year less than if the rates of twenty-five years ago were still in effect.

Western Electric

Western Electric is the manufacturing and supply unit of the System. It has been a part of the System since 1882. The A. T. & T. Company owns 99.82 per cent of Western Electric's stock, and A. T. & T. and Western each owns 50 per cent of Bell Telephone Laboratories, our research organization.

Bell Laboratories develops the finest communication equipment in the world and Western Electric makes it—for the Bell telephone companies. The telephone companies, the Laboratories, and Western work together in intimate day-to-day co-operation, and they work toward the *same* service goals. In my judgment, this three-way teamwork is the main reason why this country has the best communication service in the world, and is the absolutely essential foundation for the Bell System's success as a business.

In recent years, however, we have heard talk the gist of which is something like this:

Western Electric, it is said, is tops in the field of electronics. So its potentialities as an independent electronics manufacturer are tremendous. Therefore, wouldn't it be a good idea—and wouldn't the possibilities for profit be great indeed—if the Bell System were to "spin off" Western Electric?

Along with this talk, there has been considerable buying and selling of the very small number of Western Electric shares that are publicly held, and a steep rise in the price of these shares. If this activity in the stock is in any degree based on the notion that we might consider separating Western from the Bell System, then it is necessary to correct such a misunderstanding.

I wish to say on behalf of your Board of Directors, and with all possible emphasis, that the A. T. & T. Company has no intention of "spinning off" Western Electric either now, in the near future, in the distant future, or at any time whatsoever. The reason for this statement is overwhelming. Western Electric is vital to the Bell System. To separate it from the System would not be a mere "spin off"–it would be the dismemberment of this business and a major misfortune to our share owners as well as to our customers.

Furthermore, the truth is that Western's position in electronics manufacture *stems directly from its ties with Bell Telephone Laboratories and the Bell telephone companies.* It is the whole Bell System's drive for research that generates our technical progress, and the research gets done in the Laboratories, not in the manufacturing company. *This* is the how and the wherefore of our advanced position in the new electronic arts. And it is Western Electric's intimate *affiliation* with the Laboratories, and its *membership* in the Bell System, that makes it tops in its field.

The benefits of our research and development work accrue to our customers and share owners in two ways.

First, the new devices and systems developed in the Laboratories, and made by Western, go into the telephone companies' physical plant in a steady stream so that we can perform more services for more people and do so more efficiently.

Second, we are able to negotiate agreements with other companies that give us the right to use their inventions now and in the future. When we license them under our patents, the advantages are by no means one-way. Certainly there are great advantages to the other companies, and it is a fact that the fast-growing semiconductor industry, which did a business of about five hundred million dollars last year, owes much to licenses obtained from the Bell System. But it must not be forgotten that in exchange for our giving others rights under our patents, we can obtain rights under theirs.

We now have license agreements with about 750 companies here and abroad. Many of their discoveries are very useful to us —in switching systems, for example, including our new Electronic Central Office; in radio relay systems; in new methods for transmitting speech and data; in automatic accounting equipment that records the details of long distance calls dialed directly by customers.

Under many license agreements, we also receive cash royalties. But most significant is the exchange of rights. The rights we obtain help us to serve the public at lower cost than would otherwise be possible. They help us operate more efficiently and this benefits both customers and share owners. I couldn't say that our patent rights benefit any one group exclusively. The point is, they help the whole business and work to everyone's advantage.

In talking about the rights we receive from others, I am not in any sense underemphasizing the achievements of our own Bell Laboratories. I think we have the greatest industrial research and development organization in the world, bar none. But they don't invent everything. No single organization can do that. The great thing is that they come up with so much. And so, through direct application of their inventions, plus the willingness of other companies to give us what they have in exchange for what we give them, we can always stay out in front in our technology.

Satellite Communications

With regard to space communications, you know from the annual report that much progress has been accomplished in the past year. We have made definite and we believe sound proposals for a satellite communication system. We have the technical know-how to put these proposals into effect. We can act promptly, and there is great need for prompt action. The Federal Communications Commission has stated that the earliest realization of a commercial system is a national objective—that this may be accomplished through concerted action by existing agencies of government and private enterprise—and that in accordance with traditional policy in this country, private enterprise, under regulation, should be encouraged to develop and use satellite systems for public communication services. The Commission has also assigned to the A. T. & T. Company radio frequencies for experimental use with our proposed system. So we are ready to move. What we are seeking today, and have been seeking for several months, is for some branch of the Government to provide facilities for launching experimental satellites that we would be glad to pay for.

We would use such satellites for the same purpose that we now use ocean cables and short-wave radiotelephone facilities, that is, to connect our communication network in the United States with the networks of other countries, and thereby provide international overseas service to the general public.

We have been providing such service for thirty-four years. A satellite system would be a natural supplement, a natural extension of the means already employed. To us a communication satellite is simply another relay station. Radio signals are beamed up into space, and the satellite receives, amplifies, and retransmits the signals down to earth again.

An important point is this: A satellite communication system would have large capacity. It could provide *many* channels to interconnect our network with those of other countries. And the demand for international communication services is growing fast—very fast. Overseas telephone conversations increased 20 per cent last year. To provide ample, high-quality, dependable service in the years ahead, both ocean cables and satellites will be needed.

So we have these very practical and pressing considerations of future need. They are one reason why we have been urging prompt action. The wise thing is to take time by the forelock. Furthermore, I for one would dearly like to see this country the unquestioned leader in space communications, and I am sure I am not alone in that wish. None of us wants the United States to come in second again. To accomplish the result we all hope for, it is essential to move ahead without delay.

1962

Profits Promote Economic Growth

The fact that Bell System earnings have measurably improved over the levels that prevailed some years ago has been absolutely essential to enable us to manage a construction program that is now getting up fairly close to three billion dollars annually. And it ought to be remembered that a vigorous program of this kind, which provides employment for many thousands of people outside our business as well as inside it and opens the way to new and improved communication services that in turn enable all industry to function with greater vigor and efficiency—it should be remembered that this is precisely the kind of vital, dynamic activity that creates the economic growth the country needs. The heart of it all, I emphasize again, is a good profit, plus constant effort through research and invention to employ more efficiently, and in more and more ways of value and use to mankind, the capital that profit creates and attracts.

Taxes

There has been a revival of proposals to withhold personal income taxes from dividend and interest payments, and to repeal the fifty-dollar dividend exclusion and 4 per cent dividend credit that have been allowed on personal income tax returns since 1954.

We have never favored withholding from dividends and interest, and have repeatedly urged that at the very least, provision be made to exempt from any such withholding all investors who are not liable for income taxes and who would have to wait months for refunds of money they never owed.

We have strongly opposed—most recently before the Senate Finance Committee, less than two weeks ago—the proposal to repeal the fifty-dollar dividend exclusion and 4 per cent dividend credit. These were instituted in 1954 because it was clearly apparent that some relief from the burden of double taxation was necessary in order to induce people to place more savings in risk capital. Since that time the number of men and women who own shares in American corporations has more than doubled, and the amount of new money provided by investors, in risk or equity capital as well as in debt capital, has greatly increased. Today the need for risk capital is greater than ever. To grow and provide jobs, business in the years ahead must attract and employ many billions of dollars. What is wanted—what is necessary—what is urgent—is to offer *more* incentive to savers, not less. In our judgment a return to complete double taxation, which would discourage risk-taking investment, could cause serious damage to the economy.

Also before the Senate Finance Committee, we have urged

the need for basic tax reform. The reform we urge is that the tax laws allow depreciation expense that will fully recover the purchasing power of the investment used up in providing goods and services. Why has this country fallen behind in modernizing and expanding productive facilities? It is because so many businesses have not been able to replenish the capital eroded through high tax rates and inflation, and so have found it impossible to bring their plant and equipment up to date. This is the root reason and the ill runs deep.

Western Electric's Responsibility for Nike

The current investigation by Senator McClellan's Subcommittee into missile procurement methods has dealt mainly with the development and production of Nike missile systems, for which Western Electric, our manufacturing organization, has been, and is, the prime contractor.

In newspaper reports I have seen statements and figures that give the quite erroneous impression that Western Electric has made large profits that it did not earn. I will come to that in a minute, but first let me make a few points that somehow do not get into the papers.

The first point is that Nike missile systems are of unexampled complexity, and the task of bringing them into being has been one of the most complex management jobs any business was ever asked to undertake. It has involved basic research, mathematics, systems engineering, manufacture and assembly of thousands of different kinds of components, and weaving together into a reliable system all these elements that are themselves the product of diverse skills in communications, electronics, aerodynamics, rocket propulsion, computer systems, and other arts.

The second point is that in 1945 Western Electric was requested by the Army to take responsibility—and here I quote the language of the contract—for "production, completion, and satisfactory operation" of all elements of the Nike systems. The Army said in effect to Western Electric, "Here, you take the whole job, and we will hold you fully responsible for the result." And that is what Western has been paid for.

The third point is that Nike antiaircraft systems have accomplished with eminent success the purposes the Army envisioned. They are the first fully deployed antiaircraft missile systems for the defense of our cities. They are there, and they work.

The fourth point is in the basic question that Senator McClellan's Subcommittee is asking: Is the single-manager method of developing and producing defense systems the most efficient, the most successful, the most economical? Should the task be assigned to a prime contractor who will use the services of subcontractors, but remain the responsible manager of the whole undertaking and be responsible for the total result?

Our own view is that so far as Nike is concerned, these systems could not possibly have been created so soon, or so economically, in any other way. No one will disagree that the Subcommittee's question is important, or that objective review of past experience might help to suggest economies in future programs. But now I want to give some of the reasons why we feel so strongly that the conduct of the Nike program has been to the country's advantage, not only in Nike's performance but also in cost.

Since 1945, in compensation for the total responsibility required and discharged, Western Electric's profit on Nike has amounted to three and a half cents per dollar of sales. Contracts negotiated with the Army provided for markups on all costs, including subcontracting costs, in order to provide an overall profit to Western for the overall job it did. But markups are not specific measures of effort on specific subcontracts. They are simply a part of the procedure by which a reasonable profit allowance on the total job is arrived at.

Moreover, as prime contractor and general manager, so to speak, of the Nike effort, Western has maintained cost reduction programs that have cut the cost of deliveries by more than three hundred and fifty million dollars. *These savings are nearly five times the total profit Western has earned on Nike in seventeen years.* In fact, this is precisely the kind of result that the Government has been paying Western to accomplish.

The Subcommittee has also raised the question of when subcontracts should be "broken out," as the phrase goes, for direct procurement by the Government, without markup by the prime contractor. The thought here is that such "break out" might save money. But this depends entirely on when the break out comes. If responsibility for significant elements of a complex system like Nike is taken away from the prime contractor before those elements are perfected in design, or before their costs are brought down as they ought to be, this can vastly *increase* the overall cost to the Government. In this kind of project it doesn't take many mistakes to send total costs skyrocketing, to say nothing of the time lost. So I hope it will be remembered that a contractor who takes full responsibility must discharge that responsibility, and should be paid for doing so.

Many thousands of men and women have worked hard and well on Nike. They are proud of what they have done, and so am I, and we can all of us strongly and proudly affirm that every cent of the profit paid to Western Electric under Nike contracts has been fully earned.

Questions Regarding Communications Satellites

Why should there be a satellite system and how should it be operated? And will it be profitable? I will take these questions in order.

First, why have such a system at all? The answer is simple. It is to enable us to use microwave circuits to communicate across oceans. On land we get thousands of communication channels by relaying microwaves from tower to tower. We have been doing this for years. But we cannot beam microwaves all the way across oceans because the waves travel in straight lines. They would be lost in space as the surface of the world curves away. However, we can beam microwaves up at a satellite, which is like a tower in the sky, and the satellite can relay them on down again to a distant point on earth.

I said we have been using microwaves for years. So there is nothing revolutionary about sending them by way of satellites. This is not a revolution. It is an extension of existing arts. Moreover a satellite communication system to do a meaningful job must be tied in with the existing communication networks on land. This and this alone will enable you to send your communication from wherever you are to wherever you want it to go overseas, just as conveniently and easily as though you were calling downtown.

We want to use *both* cables and microwaves across oceans because worldwide communications are growing. Increasing numbers of transoceanic circuits will surely be needed to take care of business all over the world. As traffic builds up in the future, we see satellites as a sound way to take care of some of this future growth.

The second question was—how shall satellite communications be operated? In our view, ownership and operation of a worldwide system should be shared among all participating countries. With respect to ownership and operation of the United States portion, we are convinced the best results would flow from the international communications common carriers doing the job under public regulation. This matter is now before the Congress, and several bills have been introduced. The bill proposed by the Senate Space Committee, for example, recognizes the adequacy of regulation by the Federal Communications Commission. It would also allow ground stations to be owned by the carriers under license and regulation by the F.C.C. These are sound basic principles. However, the bill would broaden ownership of the satellite corporation, and while we do not say that its provisions in this respect are unworkable, we still believe the carriers could do the job more promptly and efficiently.

Apropos of this question of ownership, I would like to correct the widespread misunderstanding that government research alone makes possible communication by satellite. There has been much talk about the communication companies profiting from research paid for by the taxpayer. This contention has no basis in fact. Obviously, government research in rocketry makes it possible to put a communications satellite in orbit. This rocketry accomplishment is tremendous and no one would want to deprecate it.

However, it is the research and development work of private industry that makes communication by satellite possible—and also, in fact, the many kinds of information-gathering satellites put up by the Government. The transistor, the ruby maser, the solar cells, the traveling wave tube, the horn reflector antenna—all these inventions and developments are the products of private research, and in them Bell Telephone Laboratories has played a leading role. It has been well said that government-paid research provides the transportation, and industry-paid research provides the communication.

And I want to add this: In no event will the communication companies profit from the rocket research paid for by taxpayers. For one thing, that research was undertaken for other purposes and the cost incurred would not be a bit different if there were no satellite communications. Second, we are paying fees for rocket launchings. Third, whatever profits the communication companies earn from satellite communications will be regulated, and will be based strictly on their own investment of their own money. What this means, in a nutshell, is that it will not be the companies that will profit from government research in rocketry, it will be the *users* of the service who will get the benefit.

This gets me to the final point: Will communication by satellite be profitable to investors? We certainly expect it will be. Without such expectation, we would not invest the share owners' money. But I *must* make clear to you that this is going to take time. We are still in the stage of research and development. Furthermore, after the satellite system gets into regular operation, it will take additional time to build up usage to full capacity. How much time? At this moment we do not know. But the practical prospect, in our best judgment, is for no return for a few years, and then a gradual build-up so that we will come to earn a fair profit on our total satellite investment. You will also bear in mind, of course, that no matter how satellite communications are provided, this will be done under federal regulation, and there will be no more pie in the sky in the future than there ever has been in the past.

1963

Building for the Future

Getting into good position to meet future needs is just as necessary as meeting present needs well. In fact, how well we can do in any particular year depends largely on how we prepare for it.

There are many illustrations of this in our business. For example, in the years following World War II the Bell companies engaged in literally hundreds of rate cases to help meet the problems of inflation and give telephone earnings a much needed lift. These years of effort were essential to bring about our present much improved financial health. They were necessary to enable us to meet our responsibilities to customers and investors alike. But this is not the whole story. Year after year we have also worked to advance our technology and make Bell System operations more efficient. This steady technical improvement has operated in two ways. First, we have been able to keep increases in telephone rates, on the average, well below the general rise in prices; second, technical progress has led to many improvements in service—new speed and convenience, and new services that meet new needs.

So we have had rate effort and technical effort working together to keep the business strong and sound and vital and growing. These endeavors underlie our marketing progress, the betterment of day-to-day service, the work of all telephone people. This is why the Bell System has grown about twice as fast as the economy as a whole during the postwar years.

Financial Management

But there is another factor that is also important, and especially important to the share owners. I will call it simply financial management or financial judgment. This too requires keeping the future in mind as well as the present. And in exercising judgment, your directors have several things to think about.

One is that share owners like to see dividends increased, and also to see their stock appreciate in value. This is simply human nature.

A second consideration is that we have great public obligations. We must always be ready to meet public needs for service, and our business by its nature is under public regulation. Like other companies we must earn a healthy profit to do a good progressive job. At the same time, we appreciate the need to keep our overall return on investment within the zone of reasonableness.

A third consideration is directly related to what I have just said. Our growth requires tremendous investment. To expand and improve our services in the years ahead we shall need very large sums for construction. This year's construction, for example, will cost more than three billion dollars. The money for it must come from three sources—from depreciation accruals, from earnings reinvested in the business, and from external financing.

So we have all these very practical matters to consider—the desires of the share owners, the need for growth capital, and public regulation. When we put them together, where do we come out? Well, let me indicate how we *have* come out in the last four or five years.

Evidence of Progress

We have added nearly twelve million telephones since 1958 and we are now handling about forty-six million more calls each day. Long distance conversations have increased about a third and revenues from all long distance business have gone up 40 per cent. Our investment in physical facilities has increased by approximately six billion dollars. Four years ago we split the stock three shares for one and increased the dividend. Two years ago we increased the dividend again. Earnings per share were $1.12 per share better in 1962 than in 1958. In the same period the number of shares outstanding increased substantially. And investors evidently put a higher value on each share today than they did a few years back.

I think this shows that we have been striving in the share owners' interests as well as to make our service more attractive and useful to more people. The truth is that the two go together and can never be separated.

Looking back over these four or five years, our dividend payout has averaged about 62 per cent of earnings. This is generally within the range of what other high-grade, growing companies have been paying out. What we have left after paying dividends we have reinvested in the business, in revenue-producing facilities that help increase our earning power. The effect of this reinvestment on current earnings, I can assure you, has been very salutary. In fact, if we had not done this our present and prospective earnings per share of A. T. & T. stock would certainly not be what they are.

We have never made forecasts of earnings and dividends and I shall not do so today. These unsubstantiated rumors that are circulated from time to time—they do no good and I am afraid they mislead some people. The important thing is that your directors are trying constantly to do the best for all A. T. & T. share owners that they possibly can. We want to produce for every one of you the best earnings, and the best dividends, on a sound, solid, uninterrupted basis, that good management of this publicly regulated business, which has enormous public obligations to fulfill, will possibly permit. We do not want to take ill-timed, expedient, or short-sighted action that might sacrifice permanent advantages affecting the interest of all. We want to manage in such a way that the whole business, and the whole body of share owners, will continuously benefit.

Electronic Switching

There are many sides to this business of building for the future. In closing I will mention just one more. As you know we have been working for a decade or longer to develop new electronic equipment for making telephone connections. We have spent about seventy-five million dollars on this development and it represents some of the most valuable technical work we have ever done. It will introduce a new era in communications. We shall be able to offer both business and residence customers new and improved services that they will find wonderfully convenient and easy to use. We shall also be able to operate our communication network more efficiently.

I speak of this now because the time for placing in service the first electronic telephone exchange is drawing near. It is only two years away. This first office will be in Succasunna, New Jersey, and others will follow rapidly. We will then be embarked on the enormous job of replacing all our existing central offices, one by one, with these new systems. And we already have a target date for completing this program. It is the year 2000. So you see we are really building for the future.

Between now and the twenty-first century, we shall also be adding electronic features to existing telephone exchanges. This will give them added capabilities until the time when they are eventually replaced. Right now we are trying out a new electronic system designed initially to meet the needs of business customers who have private branch exchanges. With a single unit of electronic control equipment located in a telephone company building, we can handle the switching of calls for numerous PBX customers. Similar control equipment, not too long from now, will also be making ultra-fast connections for customers who use complex data transmission networks.

Thus in more ways than one, the transition to a completely electronic nationwide communication system will soon be under way. I believe it is worth present emphasis on several counts.

Promoting Economic Growth

First, progressive improvement of this kind offers the best assurance of the continuing strength and integrity of the share owners' investment. We must constantly make the services we offer more efficient, more convenient, more useful, and more used. The development of electronic switching is a good example of our determination to do this.

Second, ability to get such a development into motion, and bring it off with success, takes a great deal of money but it also takes more than money. It takes the best people we can find and a reputation for integrity and quality that will bring them to us and keep them with us. I know I am prejudiced, but in my view the 730,000 men and women who make up the Bell System constitute a technical, industrial, and service organization unsurpassed in the world. That isn't said boastfully; we always have a lot to learn and a lot to accomplish to keep up with the competition and what the country expects of us. But to competent and dedicated people in all the Bell companies, I would like to give credit where credit is due.

Finally, progress *does* depend on building the resources to move with, as well as on the will to move. This country wants economic growth. It needs economic growth. And steadily improving communication services are of tremendous importance in helping to promote economic growth. I urge again, therefore, that the policy of greatest value to the country, so far as the Bell System and the communications industry are concerned, is for government to provide the reasonable freedom and leeway that will encourage the drive for progress. I mean specifically good and improving earnings, incentives that invite the taking of risks, and an overall attitude in government and on the part of regulatory commissions that encourages doing what ought to be done, and does not concentrate on restrictions that hamper and impede. It is certainly up to us in this business to earn our own way, and make our own record that will stand on its merits. But we do need the latitude to do our job well. On this note, we pledge again that we will do our utmost to deserve our opportunities, and spare no effort to make the greatest contribution we can to the nation's economic welfare.

From Talks at General Assembly Meetings
The Telephone Pioneers of America

FROM TALKS AT GENERAL ASSEMBLY MEETINGS THE TELEPHONE PIONEERS OF AMERICA

1957

TELEPHONE progress depends on never-ending pioneer effort. The tools we use to give service are becoming more effective all the time. As we expand the telephone system we not only can serve more people, we also can do a great deal more for them. This will become even more true in the future when we get electronic switching and the new transmission systems that the scientists are working on. All kinds of new and improved services will become possible. But none of this progress is going to happen by itself. People are what it takes.

On the one hand we're going to have a bigger, more populous continent to serve; a growing, ever changing society that has more and more need for communications.

On the other hand we shall have a range of equipment that can be used to provide just about any kind of communication service.

The challenge is in how we match our human performance to the need.

We have pioneering to do in the study of markets. We must organize the production and installation of all kinds of new equipment. We must pioneer new maintenance methods. We shall need to work out rate schedules for a great variety of new and improved services. As we broaden our "line," each step calls for pioneering judgment and action all through the organization.

To begin with, what should the scope of our service be? How far should our job go?

Then with respect to any particular service—

How much investment will be required?

Will the service pay its way?

How much will the public want it?

How can we best promote it and sell it?

Which services should we concentrate on most, and in what order?

These are only examples of service questions that call for a tremendous amount of pioneering, starting right now.

Turn now from service to earnings. Here too I think we must continue to pioneer. In the postwar period as a whole we have been under very severe regulation. Telephone earnings have been much too low. For many companies, they have improved somewhat in the last few years, but they are still not up to a level which would really assure our ability to provide, over the long pull, the most and best service at the lowest price.

To a considerable extent the public have come to think that low earnings mean low rates and good earnings mean high rates. This is not true and we (every one of us) have a pioneering job to change the climate of public opinion.

A third area for pioneering is our undertaking to provide a business atmosphere in which telephone people can best realize their abilities and personal goals. This is a never-ending effort. It embraces many things. Helping employees know the facts about the business is one. Providing fully adequate job training is another. Learning how to be managers who can foster the growth of other men and women is another. We have a lot of pioneering still to do to encourage this human growth, and to keep our business in the forefront as a fine place to work.

Finally, I am thinking of our relationship with the community.

Now the community is a lot of places. It may be a small town or a big city. It may be an office building where an installer works day in and day out. It may be a state or part of a state. It may be an industry or a company or a government bureau or department which we serve.

These are all communities; and we are related to them all.

We serve some of them perhaps in a few ways; others perhaps in many ways. But by and large, as our service grows and the variety of service increases, we touch all these different communities at more and more points. Conversely, they have more and more reasons for thinking about us, and if they think it desirable, for taking action which may affect us.

At the same time, our services are increasingly mechanized. Local dialing is far advanced and direct distance dialing is also coming along fast. Yet we must be *at home in* every one of these communities, in the village, in the apartment house or office building, in the state, in the nation. And it takes us, ourselves, *as people,* to be at home. Machines are never at home anywhere; they just happen to be located in this room or that, or down in a manhole or up on a pole. Making our business at home requires our knowing the people we serve in every community, and being known by them.

I think we can use a lot of pioneering initiative in finding ways to be at home in more places. Only thus will we understand what communities everywhere expect of us, and only thus will they understand what we are trying to do.

1958

There are nearly a million of us in the telephone industry in North America and we are bound to have many differences of opinion—as between different companies, across the bargaining table, and so on. But if we look at certain fundamentals objectively, we find infinitely more to unite us than to divide us.

It also seems to me that these fundamentals are good bench marks to help us judge the meaning of events and the worth of various ideas both in and out of our business. Take for example the simple point that the more value we build into our service, the more saleable it becomes, and the more jobs and opportunity the business can offer.

Let us suppose that in all the years since the war we had made no effort to improve our service. Suppose we had not gone ahead with the dial program. Suppose we had no radio relay—no new PBX's—no color telephones or button telephones—no improvements in teletypewriters—no ocean cables—no short-haul carrier systems—and so on. Under such circumstances our service today would have fewer capabilities, it would be less attractive, and it would cost more. It would be harder to sell in good times, and much harder to sell in a time of recession. So I feel sure that the improvements we have made in past years are largely responsible for our being able to continue to sell more service today. Needless to say, this has helped to keep many more jobs filled than would otherwise be possible.

Reasonable freedom is another essential that I think we can all agree on. There are many ways to limit the freedom of a business but I shall mention only two. One way is to hold earnings down by regulation so that the business can't afford to do the things that produce progress. This is part of what has happened to the railroads, and it makes a sad story, as you well know. In our own case we have been squeezed hard in the postwar years. It has been a big task, and it still is, to get public understanding and acceptance that good earnings are vital to progress and good service. We have had some success in this but we still have more to do.

We must see to it that the public really knows us, and that the public's representatives in government are directly, fully, and honestly informed about what we are trying to do. If we are given treatment that we believe is wrong or shortsighted, we must say so and say why—and never stop working to get the situation corrected. When, on the other hand, regulators and legislators give us the means and encouragement to step up telephone progress, then we must work to the limit to justify their confidence. And I emphasize—these are not challenges to top management alone, but to every local telephone team. It takes all of us, not some of us, to earn the financial freedom the business needs.

Another way to limit freedom is to have so many rules that people can hardly move around underneath them. Any organization has to have rules. But the function of a rule ought to be to help get things done in a sensible way, and not to hinder or prevent it. We have to keep flexible because we continuously have to deal with new situations that the old rules will not fit. We have to be on our guard against applying too many rules too rigidly. It is much better to give people the chance to exercise and develop their brains. If we will do that, they will know when the rulebook fits and when it doesn't.

Likewise, excessive rules and rigidity in job assignments block progress. In some industries this has long since become a heavy handicap. In them, regardless of practical needs, only certain people can do certain things, and some people are even required to sit around and do nothing. One man has to hold the tack while another lifts the hammer, and a third must be on hand to give them both a drink of water. This is featherbedding and it must not happen in our business. I ask you to test it against your own judgment.

Does it give freedom to make progress? Does it make service more valuable to the public? Does it make it more saleable, so that more people will want it? Does it give men and women the chance to show what they can do? And if the job happens to be a defense job, does it raise or lower the heavy cost we must all pay in taxes? I leave the answers to you.

Let me refer now to another basic principle that I think we all believe in. It is simply this: We *do* depend on the business and the business *does* depend on us. If we fall short of our best, the business will fall short too. And if the business falls short, the public will surely and quickly conclude that we have failed in our public service.

To me it follows that we must be of one mind in *wanting* to solve mutual problems on a basis that will be good for the business as a whole. I do not believe, for example, that "management" and "labor" can have divergent ambitions. We cannot serve the common good by aiming in opposite directions.

It is in the very nature of things that we will have disagreements. Thank goodness that is so, because no one is smart enough to have all the answers. But we have to have the determination and perseverance to reach solutions and decisions that we honestly believe are in the best interest, not of any particular individual, or of any particular company, or of any particular group, but in the best interest of all. If we have that kind of motive—that kind of ambition—that kind of will—that kind of courage—we need have no fears for the future.

In this business, and in this whole country, we need to work for unity. We have great opportunities, but every person who does not shut his eyes and ears to the facts knows that we also have great problems. One of these problems that you and I, all of us here, are right in the middle of, is the relation between business and government.

The kind of government we have very largely determines the kind of business we have. Government can help to provide a good working climate, the kind that stimulates and encourages progress, or it can set conditions that penalize success, discourage initiative, and sap the strength and energy of business organizations.

How? You know as well as I. By driving earnings down, as I have already mentioned. By perpetuating bad taxes—the telephone excise tax, for instance. By excessive interference in business operations. By making political capital out of attacks on organizations that happen to be big. These are some of the things that can discourage business effort.

A related problem is the problem of inflation. This is nourished both by government spending and by wage increases which add to the cost of countless products and services. Yet many individuals and groups today continue to promote so-called legislative "programs" which promise all things for all men. However these same programs do not at all make clear on what basis everything that is promised will be paid for. In my own opinion they would intensify inflation, foster "boom and bust" psychology, and work a wrong on everyone—and most of all on people of modest means.

I do not ask you to take my opinion, but to make the most progress in this country, we have all got to work hard for answers that will serve the common interest. This means that as telephone people *and* as citizens we have to test our thinking in some very basic ways.

As to any political plan or program, regardless of who proposes it, I think we need to ask—

"Will it benefit the whole community, or just some people at the expense of others?

"Is is good for the long run, or will it pile up more trouble later on?

"Is is sincere, or just smart politics?"

How each of us answers questions like these is his affair and his alone. But it is vital that each of us should ask them, try to think them through, and come to the answer that best satisfies his reason and his conscience. If business and government today are interwoven—and they assuredly are—then it is self-evident that our individual lives and duties as citizens and as telephone people are interwoven also. They are not identical, of course, but they do go together. I repeat, the kind of government we have very largely determines the kind of business we have. And the kind of government any nation has depends on one factor alone—its people.

Finally, if the way we think has much to do with the way we work, it is equally true that the way we work has tremendous influence on the way others think, and on the degree of opportunity we are all given to serve the public well.

There is one basic charge on us and that is to perform with excellence. Our responsibility is to excel. Generally through the years we have done just that. Under our free enterprise system we have pioneered and provided the best telephone service in the world, and this the whole world knows. The challenge now before us is to make this *best* even better, and to let nothing diminish our ability to do so.

1959

In the years ahead this big industry of ours will grow bigger than ever—much bigger. This makes it all the more important for us to conduct ourselves and show ourselves, in each community, as people who deserve the trust and esteem of our fellow citizens. Our responsibilities are continuously on the increase—and we must measure up.

As a part of this, I think we have to become more imaginative in figuring out how to get the most value from our technical progress. Will we realize all the possibilities to the limit? Only if we explore our markets from stem to gudgeon. Only if we learn what people want and organize ourselves to meet those wants. Only if we can devise, ahead of the time when folks come knocking on our door, the services that really answer their needs. So it seems to me that with every technical step ahead, there is more need, not less, for human effort and human brains.

Another prospect is that our business is bound to face more competition and more risk. Today more than yesterday, and tomorrow more than today, we are selling optional services and conveniences. These must compete with the products and services of all other industry—and please remember that other businesses are humping along and turning out new things just as fast as we are. To get our share of the customer's dollar, we shall have to compete and compete and compete with all kinds of new and improved consumer products.

Moreover, when economic downturns come, and people feel like pinching their pennies, they can easily ask us to remove the optional features and leave in just the basic service. Clearly, therefore, the investment we make to provide increased convenience is more risky, and it becomes all the more important that we earn enough in good times to be able to stand the gaff when the going gets harder.

However I think the matter of how the telephone industry ought to earn in the future goes deeper than that. This increasing competition with other industry that I spoke of—why should we engage in it? Why should we try to come up with new ideas and instruments and systems that will serve our customers better? Why undertake new ventures? Why accept new risks?

My own answer is that we must do all these things to be a progressive industry, one that makes important contributions to the economy and to society, that is well regarded by the public, and that competent, forward-looking people want to work in. And to do our best job, we need to work in the same economic climate that makes for progress in private enterprise generally. To borrow a sentence from last year's A. T. & T. Annual Report, we cannot work effectively in one kind of climate while the rest of business is moving ahead in another. Particularly we cannot do so as our own business faces increasing competition and as our risks increase. I think therefore that telephone earnings broadly comparable with the earnings realized by other well-managed, progressive businesses in competitive industry are necessary to produce the very best in telephone service.

So far as the Bell System is concerned, it seems to me this view is an extension of long-standing policy. Forty-five years ago, for instance, Theodore N. Vail, then president of the A. T. & T. Company, said this:

"The pioneers of the Bell System recognized that telephone service, as they saw it, was in the broadest sense a public utility; that upon them rested a public obligation to give the best possible service at the most reasonable rates consistent with risk, investment and the continued improvement and maintenance of the property."

In the late 1920s, President Walter S. Gifford expressed similar views in terms often summarized as follows: that the policy of the Bell System was to furnish the best possible service at the lowest cost consistent with financial safety, to pay salaries and wages in all respects adequate and just, and to make sure that individual merit is discovered and recognized. Mr. Gifford also commented that this policy was bound to succeed in the long run and that there was no justification for acting otherwise than for the long run.

In 1953, a statement by the A. T. & T. Board of Directors said:

"It is our responsibility that the Company shall prosper. We think it all-important therefore that we furnish the best telephone service it is in our power to provide—a service high in value and steadily improving—at a cost to the user that will always be as low as possible and at the same time keep the business in good financial health." The Board also stressed that the business must provide good pay and opportunity for employees, and act always for the long run.

Thus, over a period of many years, experience and reflection have produced some very clear and consistent basic principles.

And as I reflect on the goals of our business today, I would stress not one or two but all these aspects of Bell System policy:

It makes service paramount.

It emphasizes constant improvement.

It recognizes that progress and prosperity go hand in hand.

It calls for prices no higher than they need be to assure the financial health of the business and continuing service betterment.

It is always alert to the risks the business faces.

It brings out that this is a business of people who need the incentives of good pay and opportunity.

It takes the long view.

Looking ahead, our opportunities to improve and enlarge communication services are probably greater than they have ever been. But telephone progress and in fact all progress in this country will depend on how we tackle certain fundamentals.

For one thing, I believe Americans must demand and get sound fiscal performance by their state and national elected and appointed officials. We cannot build a better life, or keep the respect of other nations, or exercise effective leadership, if we are careless or reckless in handling money, or make a habit of spending money we don't have.

In our own jobs, to realize the opportunities ahead calls for our utmost personal and private enterprise. And to encourage such enterprise a good business climate is essential. This means that to give top-flight service we must also get an understanding of what that requires. We must get it ourselves and spread it around. In this endeavor, I believe the Pioneers, by their abilities and leadership in the business, and their thoughtful participation in public affairs in their communities, will make a contribution of first importance.

1960

Economic growth is a popular and important subject nowadays. It has political overtones. There are many theories being discussed. Someone says, "Look—Russia is growing faster than we are; we must hurry up." Someone else says, "Our economy ought to grow five or six per cent a year, instead of three or four per cent." And this thought is followed by still another—namely, that we ought to grow more in some directions and less in others; in other words, our economic growth should be steered into certain channels and away from other channels.

What do ideas like this mean? What are the implications? What is at stake?

Certainly we want and must have economic growth. We can't improve living standards without it. We can't create and maintain the military strength we need without it. And our economic growth must outrun population growth if we are to achieve these aims.

Some economic theorists hold, however, that the essential ingredients for vigorous growth are greater government expenditure and more and more government control of the economy. If we accept this argument, aren't we thereby accepting the basic idea that government management *is* better than private enterprise? That government management will bring about more and better productive effort than a free economy of free people is capable of achieving? That government can run the telephone business better than we can? That government management is best for our country and best for you and me?

In sum, if we accept the premise, doesn't it push us all the way to the conclusion that a free economy should be superseded by a planned economy, controlled by government, directed by government, run by government, from start to finish?

Those in the United States who advocate that the government should beef up and steer economic growth rarely lead their arguments to this conclusion. However the late Aneurin Bevan of the British Labor Party, speaking of his own country, put it right on the line.

"We will never be able to get the economic resources of this nation fully exploited," he said, "unless we have a planned economy in which the nation itself can determine its own priorities."

This is the ultimate position boldly stated. To oppose it is not to say that large government expenditures are unnecessary. Of course they are necessary. They are necessary for defense and for many other vital purposes that only the government can accomplish for all of us. And the government will grow as the need for these things increases, just as our business must grow to meet its obligations. But it is one thing to recognize this, and quite another to favor government management of economic growth.

If we do not believe in government management, however, then we *must* believe in ourselves as free and responsible people. We must not only believe, we must act like, vote like, and be free and responsible people. The advocates of government management have done one very useful service. They have clearly dramatized the challenge to the individual. They are putting private industry to the test. What will be our response? And getting down to our own business, must not you and I ask ourselves, "How shall we as telephone people make the best contribution we can to vigorous, worthwhile growth?"

Thinking about this, let me first talk a little bit about growth as such. Is it all good? Everyone who has crabgrass in his lawn knows it isn't. Growth needs discipline. Growth must be orderly. Growth must be healthy and sound. These requirements apply in all management, whether it be by government or by a business. In our own business, if we miscalculate our rate and direction of growth, we will waste construction dollars in one place and fall short of meeting needs in another. To grow well we must understand needs, not only what they are but where they are, not only what they are today, but what they will be tomorrow.

Nor is growth only a matter of size. Figures can describe one aspect of growth. They can define enlargement, expansion, magnification. But this is not the whole story. A man really grows when his brain works, not when his head swells. Growth should have purpose. Another way to say it is that we must grow toward something, we must have goals to grow up to.

Last April I made a few comments about telephone growth at the annual meeting of A. T. & T. share owners. I said, "We must grow as a business that is regarded as alert, efficient, and always up to date. We must grow as a business that knows how to make improvements in service pay. We must grow as a business that can meet competition wherever it may develop. We must grow as a business in which ideals of service and marketing talent and zest for discovery all meet and mingle and strengthen each other."

Adding to those comments here, it seems to me that we in the telephone business are blessed in having many important, worthwhile goals that will help us to grow usefully and contribute a great deal to overall economic growth.

We have the goal of top quality—of giving people service that is better than the best they could dream of.

We have the goal of continually broadening the opportunities our business creates for customers, investors, and employees.

As part and parcel of this effort, we have the goal of meeting and beating competition all the way from the research laboratory to the customer's home or office. I put it this way because I do not think we can be one-eighth competitive, or a quarter competitive, or competitive in any fraction. We are facing competition in science, in technical development, in the services we devise and offer, in the way we price them, in our skills of marketing and salesmanship, in the character and dependability of our service every day and every hour.

We have the goal of efficiency, of devising and using more and more efficient instruments and systems; of engineering and building our facilities in the most efficient manner; of maintaining and operating them in the most efficient way.

We have the goal of constantly strengthening and improving our communication network and services in behalf of our continental defense. This is a tremendous responsibility and it becomes more important every day. I cannot put too much emphasis upon it.

We have the goal of producing earnings—profits—that will give us the means, the strength, and the will to do our job as well as possible.

Surely we have an abundance of goals for growth. Surely also, the way we grow will have great influence on the future. Let us never lose sight of the fact that our business, communications, is one of the great energizing services of modern life. All enterprise depends on it. Every community depends on it. The military depends on it. Government depends on it. Civilization depends on it.

Moreover, when we say that all these depend on communications, what we really mean is that they depend on communication people. On you; on me; on every one of us. And everything that can be said about the growth of our business and service, our competence, our contribution to economic growth, our pioneering, our will to do the best possible job, comes down in the end to a single thing: How shall we grow as individual men and women?

Will we do a great job or will we not? Not just a good job, a competent job, a satisfactory job—but a great job. The answer lies only in ourselves. I said that as an industry we have important goals for growth. I have mentioned several of them. But the most important, the most vital goals of all are the goals we set for developing our personal talents and powers; and the most important growth, and the key to all other growth, is the personal growth each one of us achieves.

1961

What makes the character of our business, and where does it come from? You and I make it. What a business stands for will never be anything different from what its people stand for. The respect it is held in will be determined by the respect *they* command as individuals and as a team. Do they have, and do they keep on getting, the knowledge they require for the job they are called on to do? Do they have the needs of the public and the good of the country deeply at heart? Can they *always* be relied on? Will they walk the second mile? Are they ceaselessly driving for excellence, for high quality, for performance that will astonish people because it is so good? Do they base their decisions and actions on what they earnestly believe is right for the long run, rather than on considerations of temporary advantage? In my judgment, the future success and progress of our business absolutely require "Yes" answers to questions like these.

Now I would like to make a few comments about Bell System character in relation to some of the things we have all been reading in the papers.

The concept that Bell System management is out to "dominate" and "control" space communications simply has no basis in fact. It is sheer imagination. Remember, this must be a worldwide system to be of greatest use, and the rest of the world will likely own more of it than is owned in the United States. So far as this country's share is concerned, the proposals that have been made will make satellite facilities available to all licensed international common carriers, on an equitable and nondiscriminatory basis. These proposals are completely consistent with President Kennedy's policy statement of last July, favoring private ownership under regulation and establishing stringent conditions to assure equitable sharing of the satellite system, and also effective competition in the manufacture and supply of equipment that the system will use. The Federal Communications Commission has full regulatory authority to enforce these conditions and has made clear that it intends to do so.

Further, we have already made plain that we have no intention of getting into the space hardware business, even if that were possible. This is the business of aerospace companies and most of the money required for a satellite communication system will be paid to them for their products and services. We are only concerned to make sure that what we spend our money for will provide high-quality, reliable service.

In building the ground station at Andover, Maine, that will be used in testing the experimental satellites, we have already enlisted the help of ninety-seven contractors and subcontractors. When this station goes to work next spring, it will contain certain basic electronic gear, such as the ruby maser, provided by Bell Laboratories, which developed and designed it. The greater part of the entire installation, however, is being supplied by others, although built to our specifications and under our supervision.

But the main point is none of these things. The main point is the point we start from, and we do not—I repeat, we do not—start from the position that our purpose in life is to dominate. Our purpose in life is to give communication service and do it well—to find better ways and do it better—to use properly and under regulation every improved means to provide growing service to meet growing needs. This is what our efforts in space are all about, and they are not about anything else. This is our character, and any other suggestion to the contrary notwithstanding, this is how it is going to stay.

It is astounding to pick up the paper and read that maybe the reason why this country is not further advanced in space communications is because of "concentration" in the field. The truth is that this country, in which private enterprise has been entrusted to develop and provide communication services, has consistently led the way. We have been the leaders and nothing can obscure this. Specifically with respect to space communications, developments achieved by our enterprise—the transistor, the solar cell, the solid-state ruby maser, the wide-swing FM receiving system, the horn-reflector antenna, and others—these are of absolutely first consequence in making satellite communication systems possible at all.

As to "concentration," Bell Laboratories' professional and technical staff represents less than 5 per cent of all the people in industry who are doing research and development work in the field of electronics and communications. It is pretty hard to match up the suggestion that concentration has held the country back in space communications, with the evident truth that a small group has done so much to move it forward.

During this controversy on space, a few members of Congress, also, have charged that the Bell System is out to dominate and control progress to its own advantage and against the best interest of the country. One has raised the cry of violation of the antitrust laws. Another has spoken of what he chooses to call the Bell System's "history of antitrust violation," and has said that to end the antitrust action brought by the Deparment of Justice in 1949, we negotiated a consent settlement in 1956 rather than defend ourselves against charges of wrongdoing.

Why do I bring up such statements on this otherwise pleasant occasion? Because if you have already come upon them, or should do so in the future, and I say nothing about them, perhaps you would wonder, "Are we wrongdoers? Were we afraid to defend ourselves? Is this really so?" I want vou to know it is not so. As it happens, I was one of the Bell System's negotiators. I fully shared the confidence of our lawyers that if the suit were brought to trial, we, and not the Department of Justice, would win it. But we weighed the cost. We weighed the energy that would have to be expended. We knew the need to concentrate attention on the tremendous service job we had to do. We concluded that in order to put ourselves back to work and get on with our job, we would recommend acceptance of the very considerable restrictions that the Justice Department insisted on imposing as part of a consent decree.

I hope you will keep a good perspective on these matters. Some of the points that seem most important to me are these:

First, as I have indicated, it is a relatively small group that has been muddying the water. Let us not run to the conclusion that all people in government have it in for us. I don't believe they do. Most of them are just as interested in finding sound, practical answers as you and I are. They are not against private enterprise. They are for it. They may often have to make some compromise with what they would ideally like to do, because that is a necessity in political life and they could not survive otherwise. But they want what is right and if they see that that is also what we want and are working for, and can be trusted to accomplish, we need have no fear.

Second, there is only one valid test that we can apply in judging our own position and proposals. This is whether or not it is good for our customers and the country. It is a little troublesome to say even such a simple thing, for it may be taken as sounding self-righteous. I pray it will not be. But I know this: it *will* be hollow if we don't act as we speak. This is why I started this talk by stressing the importance of character. If we don't have character, if we don't keep building character, then the future will not listen to anything that we say.

Third, most of us work in the biggest business in the world. And in our industry, the big companies share with the smaller ones a special characteristic. It is true we face increasing competition for many services. But for other services our customers can find no alternative, no substitute. They have nowhere else to turn.

They are frustrated, simply frustrated, if we do not serve them well —and I mean well by their standards, not by ours.

In our character there must be two ingredients. One is extreme sensitivity to the special trust that is placed in us. When other people depend absolutely on you, you have a responsibility that is absolute. There is no possibility of getting away from this. There is no way of getting around it. It is there. This is something you and I must know, feel, and live by all the time. And really living by it means to me among other things this: That none of us will ever be satisfied to accept averages, indexes, or any external test as the full measure of personal performance. In addition to every measurement we can devise to promote excellence of service, each of us, I feel certain, must carry around in his mind a personal service meter, so to speak, that is wholly his own and is always prompting him to ask, "Is this everything I should do? Isn't there something more?"

The other ingredient is humility. Our business is big for one reason only. Other people have made it so. And as we grow, let us never forget this. For it is only our constant remembering that makes the difference between power and service. Perhaps we have something of the same kind of problem, with respect to the way other people think about us, that the United States has with respect to the attitudes of people in small countries. Ours is a great and successful nation. Partly for that very reason, others are wary, critical, and sometimes hostile. But I would not draw the parallel further. While we are a big and successful business, the people are sovereign, and we are their servants.

1962

I'll center my comments tonight around a single idea. This is that in the world of today and tomorrow, we are building new dimensions in communication service.

I am thinking of new dimensions in service across the seas, in service across the continent, and most importantly for all of us, in the way we serve in each community.

Of course these new dimensions include the Telstar® satellite, which by the way is making its 665th orbit around the earth as we sit here. So much has already been said and written about Telstar that I won't talk about it at length. But I can't help voicing once more the pride and satisfaction we all feel as telephone people and as Americans.

To me the Telstar achievement is profoundly important for several reasons. It is a first for our country that has won world-wide admiration and respect. It has put the merits of private enterprise, and of real, constructive co-operation between business and government, up in the sky for all to see. It has demonstrated again that we in the telephone industry can do what we are here for; that we can accomplish great aims; that we can and will fulfill our responsibilities for leadership in communication service.

Now let's look at some other new dimensions. Our financial dimensions, for instance, in some respects are bigger than they have ever been before. In the Bell System our construction program has now moved up to about three billion dollars for 1962. This is in spite of the fact that 1962 will not be our biggest growth year by any means. Why then is the program so large?

One reason is that it takes an increasingly larger sum each year to make moves and changes in the existing plant. But this is only part of the story. The most important thing is that we have the financial strength to go ahead with improvements. We can stay on a long-range program that will increase our capabilities, make our operations more efficient, and enable us to offer services of greater utility, convenience, and value.

As everyone knows, in the past few months there has been considerable uncertainty about the general business outlook. However, because we are in good shape financially, we can maintain this big long-run program, which is certainly needed to meet long-run objectives, *and* by so doing we can make an important contribution to the country's overall economic welfare right now.

In other words, building for the future makes thousands of jobs today, both inside and outside of the Bell System. And it all grows out of the fact that earnings are a good bit better than they were some years back. This is the joint accomplishment of good management and objective regulation.

All our modernization and improvement is based, of course,

on increasing technical capabilities. Today we can meet any number of customer needs that we could not satisfy a few years ago. And in the fast-moving future, we shall certainly be able to satisfy hundreds more.

But this very situation calls for sober reflection. When your capabilities increase, one thing is certain: More is expected of you. We are constantly enlarging our public commitments to perform—giving new hostages to performance, if you please. We can depend on it that the public will require us to redeem every one.

Furthermore the public's expectations will not be satisfied by technical marvels alone. Nor do the marvels stay marvelous for long. They are soon enough taken for granted. It is only our human abilities that can not be taken for granted, now or at any time. I mean for example the ability to use the tools at our disposal with thorough understanding of each customer's needs and wishes. As technical dimensions grow, these human dimensions of perception and thoughtful judgment have to grow even more.

I repeat: The more we are capable of, the more is expected of us. The more we are challenged, the more thoughtful we must be.

If we had only a very limited ability to provide communication service, we wouldn't have to know our customers' needs anything like as well as we have to know them today. For in that case, no matter what the situation might be, we couldn't do much anyway.

But now that we *can* do so much, our obligation to really learn and know what is needed shoots way, way up. We must know our way around among our own new tools. We must create within ourselves new dimensions of knowledge about what we have to offer. We must be more and more imaginative as to how different services and combinations of services can produce the best results for each customer in every respect.

In addition, new dimensions are bound to produce some plain hard problems—downright headaches. These can be all the more serious if we don't see them in time and go all-out to solve them.

To illustrate what I mean, let me talk a minute about DDD service and all-number calling.

Today two-thirds or more of our Bell System customers have DDD service, and a growing proportion also of customers served by other companies. It represents, no doubt about it, a most extraordinary technical accomplishment. When people first use it, I think of most of them feel a great sense of wonder and satisfaction that they can put calls through so fast.

But as time goes on, and novelty wears off, public attitude changes. Failures are not condoned, nor do we have any right to expect that they should be. We have built a system that does wonders for millions of people, but we cannot shut our eyes to the fact that not all of them are accepting it as an unmixed blessing.

Information service, for example, causes big problems. We have all seen the cartoons that rib us for asking customers to dial ten or eleven digits to reach "Information" in a distant area. On top of this, continuing growth requires the change to all-number calling, and in a few places this has stirred up quite a fuss.

Now I wouldn't want to overestimate the difficulties. I think most people certainly do welcome and appreciate the advantages of DDD. I think they also realize that technical advances of this kind are essential in order to hold down the cost of service to the user. All the same, we have a job on our hands to gain better acceptance. In fact we need more than acceptance. It isn't enough that people should merely "accept" what we do. Our job is to give them service they positively enjoy. And this is no little challenge; it is a great one.

The first part of the DDD job is to make performance so invariably excellent that people will swear by it and not at it. This we have not done yet; but this we *must* do. The goal of superb service—service that is every bit as good and reliable as local dial service—such a goal is not one inch too high; we have to reach it.

Second, we must make the necessities and problems of growth better understood. The need for all-number calling is an important example. This is no whim or caprice on our part. And we haven't the slightest desire to be arbitrary. But we do have to face up to realities. We do have to look ahead and make sure that we will not fall short of meeting public needs in the future. The reality is that continuing growth in telephones, plus DDD, make all-number calling necessary. And since most people are reasonable I think they will understand this.

However we ourselves need to be something more than merely persuasive. We need to show the fullest possible consideration and understanding of how other people may feel. I know we have made careful studies. I know experience shows that all-number calling works out fine when people actually get to using it. And the last thing in the world that we ourselves would ever want to do would be to set out on a program that would hamper the service.

But we had better not get into the position of seeming to say to any person that we know better than he does what he personally likes. Sentiment and emotion are involved here, and they must be respected. Only if we respect other people's sentiments will they respect our reasons.

Maybe a good deal of this worry about all-number calling comes from apprehension about the effect of technology on human life. The impact of machines troubles many people. They have a fear of being de-personalized, of losing their identities, of seeing their names taken over by numbers, by holes in cards that whiz through machines.

This is very much like the concern that is widely expressed today about the relation between science and the humanities in education, and the need for the two to come together. And this is important—the two do need to be joined, not only in school but in all of life. The problem of harmonizing science and technology with human values is one of the central problems of the modern world. Many people would say it is *the* problem. But in any case, you and I and the work we do are right smack in the middle of it. The nature of our performance must not be seen, it cannot be seen, as evidence that the demands of the purely technical, the demands of the machine, are controlling. In everything we do, in all our effort, we must bring science and human values together.

Two thoughts now in conclusion:

First, how do our service dimensions grow, anyway? By a process of constantly testing our boundaries, getting new knowledge, putting everything we know to better use, building and selling new systems and services that will do more for more people. Our economic usefulness, our vitality, our contributions to social need, to the prosperity and welfare of the nation, are all keyed to this process.

But at the same time, we must every minute be watching our step. We in the Bell System well know that we occupy a position of great prominence and responsibility. As we widen our service horizons, still we must keep them always inside the ball park. Enthusiasm cannot dispense with judgment. And in selling competitive services, we must always sell them on the basis of their intrinsic value, and never even imply any advantage that might be deemed the result of our particular position in the communications field. In short, we must be eager beavers, but one over-eager beaver will be one beaver too many.

Finally, I think of one more dimension: the dimension of leadership. Perhaps it could be said that this is the fourth dimension of all our progress. It cannot be measured. But it is necessary to all great achievement.

I do not want to be vague here. Whose leadership am I talking about? Mine? Certainly. The leadership of all in top management? Yes again. The division and district people? Yes. But I would ask further: What mind that helped to structure Telstar, what hand that helped to build it, did not thereby contribute to the leadership of which Telstar is a symbol? And to say the same thing more broadly, there is no doubt in my mind that every telephone man and woman who did a superlative job today thereby made a unique and personal contribution toward building leadership, building understanding, building public confidence, and building a better future.

Is it asking too much of ourselves to say that we will be an organization, an industry, of people who are so competent, so progressive, so trustworthy, so human, and so considerate of the needs of others that our customers, our share owners, our government, and the public in general will always look our way with confidence and cheerfully *want* to count on us?

My answer and last word here tonight is—let us never try for anything less.

1963

We are all keenly aware that the country faces great problems and opportunities at every hand. Some may speak hopefully of a truce in the cold war, but common sense tells us we cannot relax our vigilance and preparedness even momentarily. The question of how Negro and white people shall live, go to school, and work as fellow citizens, demands good solutions in every part of the nation. The economy of the country has been moving at a fair pace, but fair is not good enough. Practical, constructive changes in taxation, which would give industry fresh resources and incentives to drive ahead, seem a long time in coming. Higher and higher wage payments induce more foreign competition and more rapid mechanization, and thereby aggravate the unemployment problem. The unfavorable balance of international payments continues to drain our gold reserves. And notwithstanding wide recognition of the need to bring the budget into balance, many people press for programs that would produce deficits year after year.

I am not going to talk on all these subjects, but it seems to me we can usefully remind ourselves that how we think and act as members of this business, and as individual citizens, is important in relation to the broad problems of the day.

Through the years we have been fortunate. We have had a steady stream of new opportunities to work on. Our research and technical development, for instance, have been very successful. They have continuously brought us new knowledge, new instrumentalities, new systems that we use to broaden our service and increase our business. Invention and innovation have been a regular part of our business life.

But I would ask this question: does innovation depend on invention? I think not. Many times yes, of course. But not always —not by any means.

More broadly, I think, innovation depends on *recognition.* By this I mean simply the ability to recognize, to discern, to *see* the facts and problems and opportunities that are always around us and close at hand.

This power to discover is not reserved to the scientist. Telephone people in every branch of the business are demonstrating this in countless ways.

The operator acts with quick resourcefulness to assist callers who ask for help.

The girl in the business office comes up with a suggestion that is just the ticket for a customer moving to a new home.

The installer sizes up a job and sees a way to do it superlatively well.

So the challenge is to each of us, a challenge to be alert, to use our eyes and ears and minds, to take a two from here and a two from there and make them come out four.

At the same time, how well we perform individually depends in great measure on how we meet another opportunity that is open to all of us.

This is the opportunity, in fact the ever present need, for good communication and understanding among ourselves. Every business needs this but we need it to an exceptional degree. Why? Because we are so much a teamwork business. We depend on each other. We need understanding between companies, between departments, between bosses and their people.

I would even say a boss becomes a good boss largely by learning to be a good communicator. And this calls for several things.

A good communicator makes clear by example, as well as by his words, that the goal of doing a better job is never out of his mind. He always means what he says. He can be trusted. His object is not just to communicate *to* people—it is to communicate *with* people. He shares his ideas and seeks those of others. He listens to what is on *their* minds. He realizes they can do their most satisfying best only when they feel they have a significant personal part in the community of thinking and effort.

I think our power to see opportunity, create opportunity, and produce the greatest satisfaction for all concerned, both inside the business and for our customers, is wrapped up in our ability to get this free flow and interpenetration of ideas.

It may be said, "This all takes time. And pressures are heavy."

True enough. But at the same time, no problem behind the

pressures will be well solved if we let the pressures themselves stand in the way of our trying to understand each other. In fact, failures of communication are sure to be the source of more pressures and apparent conflicts.

Now we know this does happen. But it doesn't have to happen. As one looks at good results and poor results, and seeks the reasons why, often the answer is:

This group, or district, or area, or whatever, had good communication and understanding. This other group, although the people in it are potentially just as able, had poor communication and little understanding.

What is the secret of those who can get and spread understanding? In my belief they are just plumb determined to *find* ways to communicate. They *make* ways to do it. Recognizing the need, they innovate to meet it.

We need communication not only to understand others but to understand ourselves. Working along with others, and chewing over their ideas, ought to produce a certain amount of self-examination. It ought to help us answer the question, "Am I turning in a performance I can be proud of? Am I using my life well?"

I would say too that this matter of looking into ourselves bears directly on how we deal with our customers.

If it has been said once, it has been said a million times, "Our job is always to deal with the customer as an individual, to meet his individual needs and wants as well as we possibly can."

And we do this most of the time; but we can surely do it better. The question is, how? I think it depends mainly on each of us asking, "What would I want if I were in this customer's shoes? How close can I come to giving service that I would consider just about perfect if I were he?"

This is the greatest opportunity we have and we have it every day. How well we meet it depends initially on looking inside ourselves.

The other day one of the companies got out a bulletin to help managers think about ways to become more effective leaders. The title of the bulletin was, "Meet the Man in the Mirror."

That is, try to realize what you are like and then ask yourself where you could do better.

Applying a similar thought here, I would say, "Look at yourself in a mirror and see if you think your treatment of a customer is just what you would have wanted."

Incidentally, I know people who have actually talked to themselves in front of a mirror and come away with some brand-new notions. I think they would back up the suggestion that sometimes a full-length mirror presentation of your own ideas to yourself can answer many questions.

But to get back to our customers—

We all know that sometimes we are unable to do for a person exactly what he wants. The means for doing it may not yet exist. Or the cost may be prohibitive. Or there may be some other valid reason. But this principle of action, to do the most we can, to come as close as possible to service that people will consider perfect, this is the right principle for us. And on the same principle, when we do not meet a customer's full hopes, and we ourselves are dissatisfied with the reasons we give, then we need to satisfy ourselves by following the matter up. There is always an opportunity here, sometimes to learn, sometimes to provoke a change that will mean better service. In either case, this is the principle of progress.

Now let me say a few words about another of today's opportunities. This is for us in the telephone business to take truly constructive and forward steps in increasing career opportunities for Negro men and women.

I realize there are many differences of view about the relations between the races. But it seems to me necessary for all of us to understand that a fundamental social change is under way. What has been in the past is no longer going to be in the future. The first need is to grasp this fact.

Second, to speak for a moment here of the Bell System alone, we have more people at work than any other organization except the Government. So the matter of how well we handle ourselves has more than ordinary significance.

The third point follows naturally. I think we should proceed in the spirit of learning, and taking, all possible right ways for action—as distinguished from the spirit of doing as little as need be, the spirit of "tokenism" as it is sometimes described.

I realize there are many factors to consider. Our service obligations are paramount and people must be able to learn how to do the work well. Job openings are not unlimited. Many Negroes have been unable to obtain an adequate education, and Negro educators tell us that relatively few Negro men have been encouraged to prepare themselves for careers in business, because they have not felt that business really offered them much opportunity. Laws and ordinances range from those that forbid discrimination to those that make some discrimination hard to avoid.

Notwithstanding these various circumstances, we have many Negro men and women in the Bell System. They share in, and contribute to, the fine qualities of our organization. This is good evidence, I think, that we can extend more opportunity, and do this with good speed, if we will, and as I am sure we must. So I simply say here, let us get on with it. We have much more to do.

You are thoughtful people. You know that today's opportunities, if we fail to grasp them, have a way of turning into tomorrow's problems, or even tomorrow's crises. Since we can count on plenty of problems anyway, let's not multiply them unnecessarily. I have talked about two or three things that are probably apparent to all of us. However, the real point is for each person to take stock of his personal opportunities day by day. This is a matter of alertness, of recognition, of looking at facts both outside and inside of ourselves, and then doing something about them. None of this is easy. Finding and using opportunity is hard work. But it is less tiresome than putting out fires, and a lot more rewarding.

Developments in Communications

COMMON GOALS FOR CHANGING TIMES

Convention of the United States Independent Telephone Association

CHICAGO, OCTOBER 14, 1957

WE have a tremendous future in this telephone industry, but it isn't going to be realized on technology alone. Transistors, computers, and wave guides, and all other things the scientists discover, are wonderful. We couldn't do without them. However, they are not Aladdin's lamps. We can't just rub a transistor and make a wish and expect it to come true. The fact is that to take advantage of our new communication tools, to realize all the wonderful opportunities they open up, requires us as managers to do a better job of managing than we have ever done before.

I am sure too that the great changes which are taking place, both outside and inside the industry, will closely affect every one of us. Nobody is immune to progress. This may be disconcerting at times but we had better accept it. Nowadays jet planes don't wind their vapor trails through any particular part of the sky. The man with the oil drill may turn up almost anywhere, and the woods are full of highway surveyors. I don't mean that every hamlet is going to be a suburb, or every pasture a factory branch. But there aren't very many places that come with a no-change guarantee. In the world we live in today, most anything can happen, anytime, anywhere.

And this, it seems to me, is crystal clear; we in the telephone business must meet these changes together, for ours is one single industry and our service is indivisible. Far more than in other types of business, the progress we make depends on how effectively we combine our efforts.

I think this has been growing on all of us year by year. The basic reason is plain and simple: none of us can serve the community and the country well without the help of the others. None of us in the long run can prosper, unless jointly and together we accomplish a fine service job. All of us need each other's co-operation in order to succeed.

As time goes along this situation tends to become more pronounced, rather than less. Distance dialing is one of the factors but only one. In more and more places we live and work in each other's laps. We mesh closer and closer together. When big customers want special services, we must jointly provide them. We share rate problems and directory problems as well as service operating problems.

Now I'm not going into a lot of detail on this subject. You know the details anyway. The big thing is that we're all working on the same job and to do it well we must co-operate. And I think we are; I think we're working together better than we ever have before, and I don't see any reason why that shouldn't continue.

Of course most of us are all in favor of co-operation when it means having the other fellow do things our way. We all like that. But in real life we usually have to settle for something less. It's a matter of give and take. No one can co-operate with a stiff neck. We have to bend a little. On the other hand, being anxious to co-operate doesn't mean that anybody ought to give the other fellow his shirt, either. I guess no one expects anything along that line. But we can always meet with good will and in good spirit and work out common problems on a sound business basis. I have full confidence that we shall continue to do exactly that.

COMMUNICATIONS TODAY AND TOMORROW

Conference on Distribution, Boston

OCTOBER 18, 1960

ONE phase of communication progress that I am certain will have great impact on marketing and distribution is the transmission of data. To broaden markets, company after company has spread out and decentralized its distribution centers. The channels from manufacturer to consumer are longer and more numerous. They carry a greater and greater variety of goods. Keeping the pipelines full takes a big share of total production. All this costs money, lots of it. Control is a difficult problem.

To help solve the problem, many companies have started to use various kinds of data-processing machines. And our new *DATA-PHONE* services make it possible and practical for many types of these machines to "talk" over telephone lines. Today we can do this at medium speeds. In the future the speeds will be much, much faster. And with the whole telephone network available, and growing more versatile all the time, businesses will be able to combine data handling and communications in whatever ways best meet their particular needs. Looking specifically at the distribution problem, managements will be able to recentralize control. This we believe will give you one of your best tools for increasing distribution efficiency in the 1960s.

Also, the time is not far off when business machines will be able to originate calls automatically as well as answer them automatically. This means, for example, that when a computer has information to send to a distant location, the computer may "lift the receiver," so to speak, by itself, tell its associated *DATA-PHONE* set what number it wants, get a signal when the call has gone through, and then "talk" with the business machine at the distant end.

Another practical possibility is to query a distant computer in data language and get back spoken answers. You could ask the questions by pushing buttons according to codes the computer will recognize. The computer has a recorded vocabulary of numbers and phrases, and as it figures out the answer it selects the particular words that will go back to you over the line—market quotations, for instance, or how many widgets are currently in stock. The advantage is that you get your answer directly, instead of on punched cards that have to be translated by another machine.

We believe also that in the future many more people will want to communicate while they are on the move. Today thousands of vehicles have telephone service that connects them to the nationwide network, but the big developments are still to come. We aim to serve millions of "mobile" telephones, not thousands. People engaged in marketing and distribution, who are on the move much of the time, would be among the first to benefit. To provide such service we badly need radio frequencies that we haven't yet been able to obtain from the government. But given the frequencies we are sure we can do the job. Eventually it is altogether possible that you could carry a pocket radiotelephone enabling you to talk with anyone else, anywhere, any time. Let us say for example that a Boston wool merchant, on his way to visit a customer, might pause a moment to call Australia and check a few facts with an agent there who happened to be off on a camping trip.

The question is often asked, "When will we have visual communication so that people can see each other when they telephone?"

I think this is surely coming, but I can't give you the date. Transmitting and switching two-way speech plus vision through the nationwide system is no easy matter. From the purely technical standpoint we could provide such service today, but the price tag would be too high for widespread use. Nevertheless the potential market is great and I am confident that improving technology will sooner or later bring the cost of this kind of service down to a level where a lot of it can be sold.

You can imagine the impact this will have on marketing and distribution. Call up your dealer and show him your shoes, your ships, or your sealing wax. Let him see how they look and how they work. Take his order on the spot. Or if you happen to be a retail merchant, show telephone shoppers the merchandise they want to see. Let me not overstate this. It may be a long time before the average housewife has a telephone she can see through. But I wouldn't rule out the eventual possibility.

More immediately, many department stores now sell from 5 to 13 per cent of their volume by telephone. The average sales ticket is higher and selling costs are lower than for in-store selling. Merchandise goes direct from warehouse to customer. I don't want to make this talk a telephone commercial, but I was asked to discuss the future of communications, and from the merchant's standpoint a big part of that future lies in this area of telephone selling.

Just a word more about seeing while you telephone. One reason the cost is high is that a communication channel capable of handling vision has to be far wider, electrically, than a channel that handles only sound. If we are going to switch see-while-you-talk calls through a network, each channel we switch to has to be a wide channel. Therefore this sort of network would probably develop step by step, over a period of years, to meet the specific needs of various customers.

And I call your attention to this: The wide channels needed to handle vision can also handle communications to and from big all-purpose computers. You see the possibility I am suggesting—the development of a network, maybe small at first, but capable of growing, that would interconnect different businesses with computer centers. Perhaps in some such way as this we shall start toward the creation of a big wide-channel communication system, over which we shall be able to switch pictures, whole rivers of data, or what have you, between any two customers who have compatible equipment.

Satellite communication systems are still in the research

stage, but we are pushing the research hard and also digging into the whole range of problems that must be dealt with to create a working worldwide system. At the same time we are going ahead with more cables, to Europe, to Caribbean points, to South America, and to Japan and other places across the Pacific. Cables and satellites will complement each other, we feel sure, in making possible the new order of global communications that we foresee in the next twenty years.

Almost every new communications development presents new opportunities to you in the field of distribution: new selling techniques, new markets to reach, new ways to speed goods to market, new methods of inventory control. And we in the Bell System are going all-out to compete for your business and your favor. We want to help you get the best possible results for your business by making good and plentiful use of ours.

Every now and then I run into a businessman who tells me he wishes there was some way the telephone company could perform such and such service for him, when the fact is we could have done it long ago if we had known his needs sooner. Now, it is certainly our responsibility to take the initiative on learning what your communication needs are and working to meet them. But if you have an idea first, a need, a wish, a problem, a question —anything at all—by all means, don't hesitate, but ask your telephone company what it can do for you. Chances are good that we can do a lot, and maybe much more than you would ever have suspected.

PROGRESS IN COMMUNICATIONS

North Carolina Citizens Association

MARCH 22, 1961

TO HELP tell my story tonight, I shall use a few key words. They are simple words but they go a long way toward describing the function and nature of modern communication systems. The first word is "control." In the modern world, millions of people and machines perform separate tasks of all kinds. To maintain orderly relationships we must exchange information constantly regardless of distance, and do it very fast. If we could not communicate in this way, we would not be able to fit things together. So high-speed, universal communication provides the essential means for organization, the means of control.

Also, there are more and more people all the time, and more and more machines. Human activities every year become more diverse and specialized. Hence communications must have increasing speed, scope, and dexterity.

In working to bring this about, we are learning many new ways to control the functioning of the communication system itself. For instance, telephone dials for many years have had controlled mechanisms that set up connections for local calls. But now the range of control is spreading way out. Turning the dial not only controls local equipment, it also selects long distance routes and then controls still more equipment thousands of miles away.

I could give many examples of the control function of modern communications. To the military, communications is the means of command, which is the military word for control. Today, merely by lifting a telephone receiver, the general officer who lifts it can instantly command forces all over the world.

Here is another example of control. When a Titan missile takes off over the missile range, or a rocket carries a Tiros or Echo satellite up into space, a communication system exactly controls the rocket engines and other equipment so that the missile nose cone will find its target, or the satellite its proper orbit. This particular system, I might add, is built by Western Electric right here in North Carolina.

Controlling objects in space is dramatic, but the control and co-ordination of machines on the ground is no less important. More and more, industry and government are using business machines of many kinds to solve complicated problems, to speed up and streamline distribution as well as production, to hold down the vast tide of paper work. And in one respect anyway, many of these machines in business are similar to the people in business. They don't work in solitude; they work together. Consequently, just as human beings need to communicate, machines need to communicate too.

The first need of a computer, for instance, is to be fed information. It has to have fodder to chew on. If you have right at hand all the fodder it can absorb, well and good. But if some of the information is miles away (and it usually will be) you don't have to get it to the computer by packing it on your back. You send it over a modern communication circuit. And I think it can be said of nearly all the machines that help us organize work, that read and analyze and compile reports and calculate estimates and results, that their usefulness increases when they can work together regardless of distance.

This is why we in the Bell System have such a strong feeling that in the foreseeable future, perhaps within fifteen years or so, the volume of information communicated between machines may be even greater than the amount of communication between people. If this idea surprises you, remember that machines can "talk" and "read" a lot faster than humans can. Right now, for example, we are developing a data communication system that will send the equivalent of about three thousand words a minute, or two or three times as many words as I have used so far in this talk.

Let me give you now a practical illustration of communication between machines, and this will lead to the second key word I had in mind.

Say you are buying an automobile insurance policy. At the insurance company's local office your application goes onto some punched cards. Then a clerk makes a telephone call to the company's home office. At each end of the line, what we call a *DATA-PHONE* data set is hooked into the connection. In a few minutes' time the data on the punched cards is exactly reproduced on cards in the home office. These are processed through a computer and other machines, and shortly thereafter your insurance policy is in the mail.

The point I want to bring out is that a regular telephone call was all that was needed to provide the communication pathway. Not a special leased line. Just a telephone call, with the data set in on the connection. And what is the key word? I would say it is "flexibility." With every line, every connection, every circuit able to handle data as well as voice, we have a system that is adaptable to a whole range of new uses.

But flexibility has other aspects too. Because we now have extremely versatile, sophisticated switching systems, today we can offer a completely new form of long distance service—what we call Wide Area Telephone Service, or WATS for short. In this case the user pays so much a month to make any number of calls over a wide area, in fact all over the country if he wishes, except to Alaska and Hawaii. Or alternatively, he may buy fifteen hours of conversation time a month. Of course, this kind of service is not suitable for everybody. It is mainly for businesses that make lots of calls to many places. But it offers a new choice. It is an aspect of flexibility.

Another new service, called Telpak, is for companies that have a great volume of communications between a few specific points. They may want Telpak for voice. They may want it for data. They may want it to transmit copies of documents. They may want it for all these purposes. The point is, they can meet many different needs by leasing what amounts to a broad communications highway. This too is flexibility.

The same concept is at work in new communication instruments of many kinds: Office and home equipment, for instance, that can be variously arranged to meet different situations. Phones that automatically dial numbers when you press a lever, and phones you can use without using your hands. And some day, I am sure, phones that will send pictures as well as words.

Now we can never get flexibility in communications just by saying, "Let's have it." We get it only by never-ending research and technical development. I mentioned a moment ago that modern switching systems are extremely versatile. But they are not nearly as versatile as the Electronic Central Office of the future promises to be. This will do all sorts of things not possible today. Just by pushing buttons, you can tell it to forward your incoming calls to wherever you wish. If someone telephones you and your line is busy, the Electronic Central Office can keep the call in mind and ring later, when the line is clear. In fact, it will do almost everything except tell you what to say. An experimental system of this kind is now on trial in Illinois, and we are well along on a model that will be produced in quantity, starting three or four years hence. Naturally it will take time to get these systems on the job all over the map. But this is what is coming, and the increase in flexibility will be phenomenal. I might say too that as we introduce these new electronic offices, we shall also be adding new features to existing systems, so that they too will be more versatile than they are today.

The third key word I shall introduce is "abundance." This is extremely important in communications, and especially so in communications for defense. We have a tremendous number of telephones here in the United States, in fact about half of all the telephones in the world. To interconnect them a vast quantity of cable and wire lines and radio relay systems crisscross the map over thousands of different routes. This abundance of different pathways offers great advantages. When you dial across the country, for instance, if all lines on one route are busy, your call will automatically shift to a second route, or even a third if that is necessary. To go back to the first key word, *control* is extended by reason of the very size and diversity of the total network. And to refer now to the second key word, you see that the total network has tremendous *flexibility*. We not only have flexibility in the switching equipment itself. We also have it because the network offers so many alternate paths.

As I have indicated, this is of top importance in communications for defense. The first essential here is that whatever the emergency in any one place, the rest of the network will continue to operate. If you have a separate communication system for defense purposes, and bombs break the thread, then communications are lost. But if you use a great multiplicity of threads, with connections between them at many points—like a spider web—then if some threads are broken, emergency communications can follow other routes. There *must* be alternate paths. Therefore, our first great asset for defense communications is the tremendous diversified network that we already have and that is growing larger and more diversified every year.

For years now we have been building new routes that bypass critical target areas, that swing around big cities in wide circles, that run for hundreds and even thousands of miles without touching metropolitan centers, and intersect other communication lines at many points to provide additional alternate paths. We use these routes for regular service every day. At the same time, they are a prime investment in national defense.

Building on this foundation, we are going ahead with a continuous program to strengthen and protect the system further. One current project is a deep-buried cable across the country, with underground offices along the way. Other projects are in the study stage. The defense problem is always changing and developing. We are keenly aware of this, and are acting accordingly.

Before concluding I would like to take a quick look at the long-range future of communications and its relation to economic growth. For convenience, some of the likely developments might be put in two broad categories.

First is complete mobility for personal communications. This means telephones in millions of vehicles, for example, instead of the relatively few thousand that are equipped today. A telephone for your car would be as commonplace as power steering, though probably "optional at extra cost." Further, for those people who might some day want to carry a personal telephone in their pocket or handbag, I think it altogether possible that they will have them, though I couldn't give you the date.

The second category is even broader. Today most people use telephones only for talking. But as we have seen, data services are beginning to add a second dimension. See-while-you-talk service will add a third. The problem here is simply the cost. To send a TV picture from here to there, we need a circuit, a communication channel, far wider, electrically, than a channel that handles only speech. These wide channels are expensive. And to switch see-while-you-talk calls through a network, every channel we switch to has to be a wide channel. Therefore this sort of network would probably develop step by step, over a period of years, to meet the specific needs of customers who would find the result well worth what it would cost.

But in time we will find ways to get the cost down. And as we do, it is not hard to visualize the impact this will have on everyday life. Many of you ladies here tonight may be able to see what you buy when you shop by telephone. Almost certainly your daughters will. And they and their families will be able to visit museums by telephone, take study courses by telephone, and perhaps some day even call the library, ask for books and reference materials, and read them by telephone.

Businessmen will be able to see, talk with, and exchange written material with their associates, without everybody going to the same place. Of course people will always be on the move. But traffic jams and commuting problems will be greatly reduced. Periodicals and even newspapers may be delivered over telephone lines, to be printed on reproducing machines in homes and offices. Sales managers will display their firms' goods to sales representatives all over the country.

Progress in communications will promote economic growth by helping all industry to control costs and increase efficiency. It will help the cause of education on which the whole future depends. It will help solve the problems of population density and the crowding that troubles our cities. It will help people make better use of leisure time.

Just one other thought before I close: The discoveries that produce progress in communications generate progress in other fields as well. The transistor is an excellent example. This was invented at Bell Telephone Laboratories in 1948 as the result of intensive research in solid-state physics. Today we are using transistors and an ever growing family of related semiconductor devices to give the telephone system new capabilities. We use them in the switching devices that make possible direct distance dialing, and in lots of other ways. And this new technology provides the foundation for the Electronic Central Office that I mentioned earlier.

Missiles and satellites also rely on solid-state electronics. Nike Zeus, the anti-missile missile system that Western Electric and Bell Laboratories people are now working on, is only possible by reason of new devices of many kinds. In literally hundreds of ways, this new art has become indispensable to the nation's defense.

Moreover a new industry has been born. Already it employs thousands of people in many companies from coast to coast. I am speaking here of companies outside of the Bell System. Last year the semiconductor industry in the United States did a business of some five hundred million dollars and in years to come it will be much bigger than that. In fact, an estimate has been reported that by 1970 the country's electronics industry, firmly based on solid-state technology, may be turning out an annual product of twenty billion dollars.

Now this is what I call economic growth. It is growth that comes from creative energy and enterprise. This to me is the right way, the sound way, the sure way, to economic growth. For the benefits flow back and forth and in all directions. From the energy and enterprise of others, the innovations, the flow of ideas and the broadening of skills, we in the Bell System draw great benefit. And from our ideas, our discoveries, our creativeness, we believe others benefit likewise. If we all give the most we can, the very best we have, to the development and improvement of our own enterprises, the value is bound to spread. And in the process, each of us in the long run will get back, from the sum total of everybody's effort, more than he gives.

Economic and Public Affairs

PRIVATE ENTERPRISE AND PUBLIC AFFAIRS

The Bond Club of New York

NOVEMBER 20, 1958

LONG ago it was remarked that everybody talked about the weather but nobody ever did anything about it. Nowadays everybody talks about inflation, but few of the efforts to do something about it have had conspicuous success. Ideally, if inequities in taxation were eliminated or minimized, the overall tax burden on business reduced, and individual incentives restored, I think gains in productivity would accelerate, we would have much less inflation of prices, real wages would increase, business would do more business, and government revenues would be greater.

Maybe not every economist would agree with that statement, but I know some who do, because I asked them to read it before I said it and they gave me a green light. Moreover, my observation is that government is just full of able, hard-working, and reasonable men who have much the same fundamental thoughts. As a practical matter, however, circumstances press them hard. They must read the wishes and attitudes of their constituents, which they are in no position to ignore. It is difficult for them to act always as they would most deeply and personally desire. And I think we in business have added to their difficulties by failing to expose ourselves, our ideas, and the facts at our command in ways that win widespread belief.

All of us hear more and more these days that business should throw off past restraints and "get into politics"—to put that phrase in quotes. It is a phrase that can be interpreted in different ways. One interpretation, and a good one, is that businessmen as individuals ought to be more active in public and political affairs. I'll say a word about that in a moment. First however let me comment briefly on another interpretation which seems to me dangerous. This is that with labor already in there pitching to get candidates nominated and elected, business, as such, had better get going and do the same.

I think this idea can do great harm. In the long run I think it would fail even if it were to have some immediate success. The reason it would fail is that any time the people of this country decide that their elected representatives have been maneuvered into office by a particular group, be it organized business or organized labor, they will, and they should, vote them out. It may take a little time, but it will happen.

What then should we in business be doing about these things? How can we bring about better relations between ourselves and our representatives in government? What is our proper responsibility in public affairs? How shall we increase public understanding of the problems of industry, and confidence in our determination and ability to serve the public interest? I shall mention four points.

Number one in our business, and I would assume in any business, is that we simply must do the best possible job for the people we serve. I know that sounds obvious and I am sorry if you think I am being trite. But we can never, never forget this. In my humble opinion, it must always be the first thought in our minds.

The second point I tried to express when I was talking to a group of telephone people a couple of months ago. I said it this way:

Doing our best is not enough. We must also tell our story and tell it convincingly. We must do this in every community. We must see to it that the public really knows us, and that the public's representatives in government are directly and fully and honestly informed about what we are trying to do. If we are given treatment that we believe is wrong or shortsighted, we must say so and say why, and never stop working to get the situation corrected. When, on the other hand, regulators and legislators give us the means and encouragement to step up progress, then we must work to the limit of our ability to justify their confidence and their trust.

Let us once and for all get over the habit of going to people in government when we need something, and ignoring them when we have nothing to ask for. Let's never ignore them. And I mean never. Let us rather, as their constituents, invite them on all suitable occasions to tell us what they have been doing. Let us invite them also to see what we have been doing. Let us tell them our plans and take a sincere interest in theirs. Let us by all means increase our understanding of their problems, as we hope they will gain insight into ours.

To do this will not of itself settle anything. Nor do I think it should. But if we in business are the kind of people we ought to be, then it ought to be good for people in government to know us as we are. In addition it ought to foster more interest in government on the part of more people in business.

This last is really my third point. I said earlier that I thought business should be very wary of taking the same kind of leaps into politics that labor is taking. But I certainly did not mean that businessmen as citizens should lie down and play dead. On the contrary, business and especially big business has been criticized, and it seems to me with justice, for making it difficult for people in management to take part in public affairs. The net result, says the criticism, is that far too many of us, managers and employees alike, are politically inert: we have little or no idea of what democratic government is all about or of what the duties of citizenship are.

I am not talking about running for office and holding down a management job at the same time. Though there may be exceptional cases, generally the two do not mix. I think it might be difficult, for example, to be the mayor of a city and at the same time manager of the local telephone exchange. On the other hand, there will be situations where there is no possible conflict of interest, and one person can handle two jobs well. Circumstances alter cases. And quite apart from officeholding, I see every reason for encouraging people in business to engage in political affairs, as individual citizens, and no possible reason for discouraging it.

Now I'll come to my fourth and last point. Recently in an article on foreign affairs I read this thought—that today, 80 per cent of the population of the world is having a brand new experience. For the first time in history, they are waking up to the fact that the price of rice is related to the kind of government they have.

I wonder how many men and women in American industry really understand *how* the price of rice is related to the kind of government *they* have and the kind of government they vote for.

Do they know that how well their industry can serve *their* interest depends on how well it can serve the interest of *all?*

Do they know that this depends, in turn, on the freedom their industry is given to prosper?

Do they know that a healthy economic climate depends on the political climate their votes establish?

As to any political plan or program, regardless of who proposes it, do they search out the answers to questions like these:

Will it benefit the whole community, or just some people at the expense of others?

Is it good for the long run, or will it pile up trouble later on?

Is it sincere, or just smart politics?

I do not at all underestimate the intelligence of people in industry. I think they are well able to look at the evidence and decide. But I think they have not always had all the evidence. In fact, sometimes the evidence about boils down to each party trying to promise more than the other. And while I am dead against corporations engaging in partisan support of candidates, I certainly think we should do the most we can (and that is more than we have been doing) to discuss policies and issues and call attention to their impact.

I hardly need to say how foolish it would be for any business to work along these lines on a merely self-serving basis. Only our own conviction that we speak in the public interest will create conviction in others. But if we have this conviction, and speak with courage, I am confident we shall be performing a public service and that our efforts will be so recognized.

CREATING A CLIMATE FOR BUSINESS GROWTH

The Southern Governors' Conference
Asheville, North Carolina

OCTOBER 13, 1959

EXTRAORDINARY change and progress have marked the life of the South in the past two decades. An economy formerly based on agriculture has become more and more industrial. People have moved away from the farms and into better-paying jobs in factories, service industries, and office work of all kinds. You have seen rapid population growth in metropolitan areas. Improvement in per capita income has been remarkable.

Moreover the forces now in motion promise even more change in the future. One such powerful force is population growth. The likelihood is that by 1975, hardly more than fifteen years from now, there will be some sixty million more Americans than there are today. Of this total, perhaps fifteen million will be here in your states.

And in what sections of the states will they be? On the farms, very few. In metropolitan areas, the great majority. For the mechanization of agriculture is bound to continue also, and as it proceeds there will be fewer and fewer farm workers. In short, as your total population keeps going up, your farm population keeps going down.

Good Cities Need Thriving Industry

This means that your cities and their suburbs will *have* to grow. It is not a matter of choice. It is a matter of necessity. And to have good cities, flourishing cities, cities in good health economically and socially, you will need to develop and diversify your productive resources far beyond what they are today. You will be called on to expand and expand and expand all the various attributes of an urban, industrial society—school systems, highways, factories, homes, parks, hospitals, libraries, utility services, and all the rest. And in every case, the ability of the community to create and support all these attributes will depend most of all on the ability of industry to thrive.

Why so? Because there is no other source of wealth that can pay the costs of urban progress. Only industry and commerce can produce the wealth you need, and only if they are given the opportunity and encouragement to do so.

In the last twenty years income per capita in the South has more than doubled, taking into account the change in the value of the dollar. This has been a magnificent performance, well ahead of the relative improvement for the United States as a whole. However, per capita income in this region is still well below the national average.

So your need is plain. It is in the word I have already used. Your need is for more wealth. Not in the sense of a few people sitting on bags of gold. But wealth, just the same. And the one way to get it, in the amount you require, is from industry that will produce goods and services, create markets, provide good jobs, and pay taxes.

Of course you know this. The chambers of commerce all know it. Your industrial development commissions know it. So you go out and promote what you have to offer—and you have a great deal. Good sites for industry, fine people to work in industry, natural resources, climate, power, transportation facilities. Grade-A communications, too! In short, all the attractions you can wrap up in a package to magnetize new industry and pull it your way.

Needed—Opportunity for a Fair Reward

Now I fully agree that all these things are important. They are very important. I wouldn't underestimate any of them for one minute. But in my judgment all these things together are not worth the cost of a single development commission ad in a business magazine, if you cannot or will not give industry the confidence that in your state it will have full and fair opportunity to earn a good reward.

Certainly it is no part of your responsibility to guarantee reward. No one can do that. No one should even try. I am well aware too that for businesses operating only partially in the South, and competing in nationwide and worldwide markets, many other factors will affect their success, in addition to the political and economic climate they encounter here.

Nevertheless, insofar as they do operate here, invest capital here, sell goods and services here, pay taxes here, and assume all the responsibilities of corporate citizenship here, they expect, and it seems to me you can take it as an axiom that they will always expect, a business climate that will be helpful and not obstructive.

They will look for a basic understanding by political leaders that good profit is essential to enable any company to expand and provide more jobs.

They will look for legislators and executives who think and act on the understanding that only profitable business can pay the taxes needed for state services.

They will look for governors and mayors and county and parish managers who genuinely want to see business succeed so that the community can grow in well-being at the same time that it is growing in numbers.

Moreover they will look for these attitudes everywhere—South and North, East and West, all over the map. And wherever a business contemplating expansion goes exploring, just about the first thing it always does is examine the businesses already there.

How are they doing? Do they like it or don't they? Is the answer headaches? Or is it hurrahs?

Also, what about utility services? Are they abundant and good? Are the utilities themselves working in a business climate that encourages them to go ahead? Or are they being held down and held back? After all, the status of the utilities, which are regulated by government, is one of the best barometers of government attitude and political climate.

Encouragement vs. Restriction

If my own judgment were sought regarding where to move a business, or expand or start a business, I would have plenty to say in favor of many parts of the South. However there are a few of your states that I would not feel like recommending. Why this lack of enthusiasm? It is simply because, in these states, our experience in the telephone business has been discouraging. If other businessmen were to have the same kind of experience, I think their reaction would be that government was more interested in curbing enterprise than in expanding it; more interested in preventing or limiting profit than in getting benefits from it; more interested in keeping capital away than in attracting it; more interested in discouraging effort than in stimulating it.

Yet these cannot conceivably be the true attitudes of, let us say, regulatory commissions and their staffs. And I hardly need to say that I know they cannot be your attitudes. I can only conclude, therefore, that in those places where regulated industry is compelled to operate at bare subsistence levels (and they are not all here in the South) we in the industry have failed to gain good understanding by the community of what it takes to serve the community well. The essence of this in my judgment is good profit, and if you will permit me, I should like to name for you briefly some of the reasons why I hold this opinion.

In the first place, only a profitable business can generate or raise the capital that will enable it to grow, produce more goods, hire more people, and pay improving wages. Only a profitable business can pay for research and development work to improve its products and services, create new ones, and reduce their cost and price.

Not only is profit a measure of efficiency; good profits actually promote efficiency by enabling a business to plan and invest soundly for the future. Where heavy plant investment is required, the financial ability to engineer and build in the most efficient increments makes possible important economies. Short-range piecemeal construction, in contrast, when a business is pinched for money, results in higher unit costs and requires more capital in the long run. This of course makes for higher costs of operation and higher prices.

Again, the profit incentive stimulates imagination and the desire to provide better goods or services. If the telephone company, for instance, develops an optional service with special features, people may be willing to pay a premium for it. The test of the market will decide this. If the project is successful, the company may increase its overall profit. Thus several gains are accomplished. Customers who elect to buy this optional service get something they want. The company improves its financial situation. Most important also, the company is encouraged to try another new venture.

But now let us suppose that just because this little success the company has had has increased its profit, the state commission comes along and orders the company to reduce its profit by cutting its rates. I could give a lot of reasons why I think this is bad, but at the moment I shall give only one: It has a deadly effect on the desire of people to dream up and work out new improvements. If the inevitable result of coming out with an attractive new offering is that you run smack into a rate cut, then why make the effort to come out with another? In two words, why bother? And the sure way to wind up with a dull business, of dull people, with a dull future, is to tie the business down so it won't bother to get up.

I spoke a few minutes ago of industrial development commissions. I guess by now nearly every state has one. And in each state government the development commission occupies a certain corner, niche, or pocket—whatever you want to call it. But I ask you, gentlemen, is it a wise or effective thing for this particular branch, arm, or finger of the state to be straining to attract business, while at the very same time another arm or finger is planning or executing some decision or procedure that will have a precisely contrary effect?

If industrial development is important enough to justify a commission to encourage it, doesn't that mean that it must also be important enough for the whole state to encourage it? Why shouldn't everybody in the government—every department, every commission, every individual, every legislator, every executive—why should not *all* have similar goals? Why isn't the whole state apparatus in effect an industrial development commission?

This may be what most or all of you feel you are really shooting for. If it is, I can only say that I think you are absolutely on the right track. To encourage you further, let me give further emphasis to two points.

The Value of the Industry Already Here

One is that I hope you will go as far as you can in judging the true value to your economy of the industry you already have. You all know the story of the fellow who searched the world over for diamonds and finally found acres of them in his own back yard. It seems to me this story has real meaning here. For example, the Bell System, which has been working in your back yards for quite a while, has invested some four billion dollars in this sixteen-state region since the end of World War II. This equals the investment made by, let us say, four thousand million-dollar businesses attracted here by your various state development commissions.

Or we might imagine thirteen hundred new businesses (attracted by the commissions) each paying out a million dollars a year for wages and supplies, for local and state taxes, and for services of all kinds. This total would about equal the $1,275,000,000 that the Bell System expended in this region last year.

This is not to suggest that dollars are any substitute for performance. And I'd like to repeat—we in the Bell System are here to labor and serve. Our duty is to invest wisely, to serve well, to charge fairly for our services, to pay good wages, and to spend with prudence. But I do wish to emphasize the point that what you have now can be just as important as what you may be searching for; important today, and also important in the future. For we too want to work with you and grow with you in the years to come.

I have used my own business as an example because I am familiar with the figures. When we consider the contribution made by regulated industry as a whole, or by any broad segment of industry in the South, or by all industry that is already here, the point is even stronger.

I also believe the attention and encouragement you give to the industry you already have will have a lot to do with the character and quality of the new industry that comes here or gets born here. Let's take it for granted that what you want in your states is the best. You don't want second- or third-rate outfits, fly-by-nights, or anything of that sort. You're trying to establish new assets, not new liabilities. I don't mean that you want only established, seasoned businesses. This country doesn't grow that way. You will want new ventures too, and people who take new risks. But in every case, you want human beings of character and ability who really have what it takes to build and operate enterprises that create wealth and make a solid contribution to the community.

These are the very people who in my judgment will take the keenest look at what you have here now, and the kind of business climate you offer. Those who can do the most and contribute the most will also expect the most. And the more you have to give them, in full opportunity to earn a proper reward, the more they will surely give the South.

WHICH WAY TO SOUND ECONOMIC GROWTH?

The Economic Club of Detroit

FEBRUARY 20, 1961

WHY is economic growth desirable? Why is it important? Why is it necessary?

Economic growth is important to our country's position in the world. It is important to our morale, to our confidence in ourselves. But even more essentially, we need it so that people will have a better life. Partly this is a matter of material well-being. However, the nonmaterial aspects are of equal consequence. Economic growth pays for education. It pays for government services. It makes leisure possible. It gives men and women the chance to broaden their personal lives. In fact, we can state the need for economic growth much as we describe the need for growth in an individual. How do you measure a man's vitality, his value to himself and to others, the promise he shows for the future? Largely by your sense that this is a man who is growing and will keep on doing so. If he has stopped growing, you know with regret that you have to write him off. In the same way, if we do not have economic growth, we are on a dead-end street.

Looking at the business I am in, I feel I must constantly ask, "Are we doing the right things to contribute to economic growth? Are we creating and expanding services that promote the general welfare? Are we setting goals that spur us to that end? Is our research and development program soundly organized, and is it fruitful? Are we making ourselves continuously more efficient? Do our labor agreements promote or hamper progress? Are the people in the business getting the opportunities they are entitled to, the challenges that capture their interest, and the rewards that befit performance?"

These are too many questions to answer at length after lunch, but let me hit a few high spots. Take for example basic research. The Bell System began to do research back in the nineteenth century; we started an organized program more than fifty years ago; and we have been pushing it ever since. All modern communication systems derive in large measure from that continuing effort —from the development of basic theories of transmission and switching, and the creation of electronic devices and networks. Another fundamental theory, well known today as information theory or communication theory, enables us to measure the relative efficiency of any communication system and plan our developments accordingly. Still another basic concept or discovery, the understanding of thermal noise, underlies our ability to communicate through space via relay stations in satellites. Basic research in solid-state physics has produced the transistor and an ever growing family of new devices. Out of them we are now building totally new systems that will make possible many new services. Out of these also has come the transistor industry, already doing a business of five hundred million dollars a year with more to come.

I give these examples because I am convinced that basic research within industry, rightly organized and conducted, does pay off. If more industry had more of it, we would have more rapid economic growth. Certainly it costs something, but the cost is not prohibitive. The truth is that basic research is a small part of total research and development costs. And in any case, basic research that really produces will cost infinitely less than expensive development of the wrong things.

Now the question of profits: To me this is central to the problem of getting good economic growth. It is central because profit creates investment capital and without this there can be no growth. Generally profits have been squeezed in the last decade. If this continues, I think the country is in for real trouble. In the Bell System our most severe squeeze came in the first ten years after the war. More recently, however, we have been able to get the profit up to a better level. If we had not been able to do this, I don't see how we could possibly measure up to today's job, or tomorrow's.

Also, there are a lot of people working in the Bell System, and outside our business too, people who supply us with goods and services for whom there just would not be jobs available if our profits were back where they were in the late 1940s and early 1950s.

Now that I've touched on employment, let me say a little more. No business will contribute to economic growth if it doesn't make itself continuously more efficient. The Bell telephone companies, for example, with about 50 per cent more employees today than at the end of the war, are serving nearly three times as many telephones. There are more jobs, yes—about two hundred thousand more; but each job today has behind it some forty-one thousand dollars of investment, nearly three times as much as fifteen years ago. This investment is represented by increasingly efficient tools and systems, and so we can give much more service, and of better quality, at prices that attract more customers. This to my mind is the essence of growth.

We expect that in the long run telephone employment will be higher than it is now. However, there will doubtless be more of some kinds of jobs and fewer of others, and we also expect that there will continue to be short-term ups and downs in the number of people at work. Jobs and ways of working can't stay fixed or frozen. That would create impossible situations.

For example, if we had the same number of operators per ten thousand telephones today that we had when dial service started, about forty years ago, and if all connections were still made by hand, we would need about a million operators right now. Also, since girls have a way of leaving jobs to get married, we would have to employ about a quarter of a million new operators a year and spend a hundred and eighty million dollars a year for their initial training alone. But of course this couldn't happen, because we couldn't sell 1920-type service in 1961 at the price we would have to charge to pay our wage bill. In short, we would have neither the customers nor the jobs we have today.

At the same time, the human problems produced by technological advance profoundly challenge every management. We have to have efficiency and we have to keep increasing it. But if technological advances and rapid industrial change produce human distress, this will seriously interfere with economic growth, and the measures taken to alleviate hardship may interfere with it further. For instance, some of the current proposals for dealing with the problems of distressed areas, whatever else they may accomplish, will not use resources in ways that produce maximum growth. Yet no political party, Democratic or Republican, will fail to take political action if it appears that industry is not doing the job public opinion will demand.

Our task in part is to manage change with forethought and care; to match our hiring to the needs of tomorrow as well as the needs of today; to prevent abrupt dislocations; to anticipate the direction of changes in force composition; to devise the new forms of organization that will be needed; to develop the human skills called for by new kinds of jobs.

But we must go further. We must improve the whole tempo of economic life. This requires more acute discernment of consumer wants. It requires constant and responsive innovation in products and services. It requires intelligent use of profit and all capital funds. It requires diversification of industrial activity in the community, so that people can seek more outlets for their energies and skills. Finally, it requires labor agreements that spread the benefits of automation among all groups, and price goods and services into the market instead of out of it.

So far as the Bell System is concerned, we are going all the way to turn out an abundance and variety of service that will go far beyond anything we have been able to do up to now. We intend to give this country such quality and quantity of communications that business and government and everyone all over this land will find it impossible not to use them to ever-increasing advantage. You are going to find that the means for communicating all forms of intelligence—words, pictures, documents, data of all kinds, *everything*—will surpass anything you have ever dreamed of. This won't happen in five minutes, but we shall work at it and work at it and work at it and we *will* bring it about. Our job, our mission, is to put services at your disposal that will help you exceed your own best expectations in your own enterprise. We are sure these services will increase the efficiency of all business, reduce costs, help strengthen profits, and lead to better values for consumers. We are not going to be satisfied to give you anything less.

REALISM IN ECONOMIC LIFE

Commonwealth Club of California

DECEMBER 1, 1961

THE subject of space communications is only one aspect of a much larger subject—I mean the many-sided problem of government-business relationships. I have a great hope that in this satellite venture, the communications companies and government will be able to work together in a truly constructive way, and give a practical demonstration that they are not at cross-purposes. Equally, I have the conviction that government and business generally must seek out and use all available means to learn from each other and deal realistically with the great economic problems and opportunities of our time.

President Kennedy has taken pains to emphasize that he and his administration are not anti-business. The force and sincerity of this position seem perfectly clear to me. As the President has also brought out, the Government is dependent on business progress for the realization of national objectives. And the general economic theory of this administration, as I interpret it, looks to the power of enterprise to develop ever expanding national resources. In such circumstances, I am sure the administration has no wish or reason to defeat its own purposes.

Starting with such a view, where do we go from there?

Today the country looks forward hopefully to greater industrial production; to an increase in business spending for plant and equipment; to higher employment and a reduction in the rate of unemployment; and to a higher overall level of personal income.

These are some of our most important near-term hopes. However, I sense that many people in government, as well as in business, share a deep concern regarding certain long-range fundamentals. We have big problems and we must deal with them in a big way.

We must solve the problem of the wage-price spiral, which has plagued us for years and remains a constant threat to the economy.

We face the sure prospect of increasingly aggressive and effective foreign competition in both domestic and world markets.

We must improve our system of taxation, which now hampers vigorous personal and corporate performance. The existing tax structure has, I am afraid, greatly weakened the incentives of many people. Also, it has become impossible for corporations to recover their true capital costs in depreciation charges. The net result is that taxes on income have in fact been consuming capital—a process that destroys part of our resources and stunts economic growth.

Another basic concern is that the position of profits in the economy has seriously deteriorated. This year, when the Gross National Product will be nearly a third larger than in 1955, corporate profits will be no more and may actually be less, notwithstanding the fact that share owners' investment has increased. Furthermore, an appreciable portion of these profits must be used to make up for inadequate depreciation allowances caused by inflation.

The profit squeeze, if it persists, is a clear and present danger to economic growth. It will stand in the way of full utilization of the country's human as well as material resources. For example, even assuming an increase in business investment in plant and equipment, what will be its nature? As labor costs rise, more and more investment tends to be, inevitably *has* to be, for modernization and improvement. The tendency, perforce, is increasingly to substitute capital for labor. Hence, to the extent that increased plant investment reflects the necessity for reducing labor costs, it is not of any immediate help in bringing about higher levels of employment. Or to put the whole matter more bluntly, the tighter the profit squeeze, the tougher the problem of employing everyone who needs work and wants to work.

It is not to be expected that when the administration says it is not anti-business, everyone in government will then demonstrate some ready-to-hand, uniform amiability, no matter what. Just as in a big corporation I want to see people thinking for themselves, so in government, which is far larger than any corporation, and has more responsibilities, there are bound to be, and ought to be, many views on many subjects.

At the same time, what is necessary for good progress is a certain broad and steady consistency. The prime requisite for sustained economic advance is reasonable continuity of policy within broad limits. If you cannot tell what is coming next, from what agency or from what governmental authority, you cannot even guess what your first step should be, let alone the next one. I greatly hope therefore that the administration's declarations will have widespread influence on people in government as well as on us in business, and will serve at the very least to minimize anomalies and contradictions.

In conclusion, I would like to state a personal point of view about the economic process. There is a popular theory which, if it would only work, would go a long way toward solving everything. It is based on what the economists fondly refer to as "increasing productivity." I believe this exists all right, but I do not know how to measure it precisely, or to measure what creates it. Neither, I believe, does anyone else. At all events, each year under this theory, increasing productivity should enable industry to create another inch or so of elbow room—room to pay higher wages, absorb costs, keep prices at levels that spur consumer demand, and thus establish the economic tempo required for fuller and fuller employment. Further, in the framework of this theory, it seems natural to introduce the appealing idea of voluntary restraint—restraint on the part of business to keep prices from rising, restraint on the part of labor to keep its demands inside the elbow room.

But what we need in economic life is realism, and to me this is not realistic. The facts are that prices are determined by competition and/or regulation, profits have deteriorated, wages have not stayed inside the elbow room, and employment is incomplete.

What then would be realistic? I will make a few suggestions.

It would be realistic to begin with the idea that in a market economy, markets do determine prices, and often more drastically than the highest degree of self-restraint.

It would be realistic to abandon the notion that "productivity" increases with clock-like regularity, and that we can let the calendar, rather than the facts of life, be decisive in wage agreements.

It would be realistic to cease putting up unrealized, uncertain, and hypothetical future gains in "productivity" as collateral for today's commitments.

It would be realistic to recognize that gains in profits are as important to economic growth as gains in wages, and that the sacrifice of profits in order to increase wages and hold down prices will simply retard that growth.

It would be realistic to lift and hearten the spirit of enterprise by tax reform designed to increase individual incentives.

It would be realistic, in my view, for people in government to make themselves the forceful advocates of private enterprise, to encourage and stimulate it, to stir zeal and enthusiasm in its behalf.

Am I going too far here? Does this sound strange? I think not. It is never enough to be not against something—to go places and get somewhere you have to be *for,* you have to push and spur and encourage. What is it that makes for growth? What increases productivity? I say it is enthusiasm, drive, determination, the will to achieve. Every one of us who manages or helps to manage a business knows that success depends utterly on human qualities that must be nourished and enriched, and on giving credit and rewards wherever they are due. The success of industry as a whole, and the attainment of national economic objectives, depend on these same factors.

To say this is not to ask for favors. Government must govern, taxes must be levied, laws must be enforced, and justice must be done. Moreover, business is just as responsible as government for producing first-rate social as well as economic results. But industry needs the freedom to commit itself, to unleash all its energies, to act with confidence and daring. So I say, let government get *with* private enterprise, heart and soul, and give it the room to drive ahead. I am confident the results will be good for the nation.

BUSINESS PERFORMANCE IN A POLITICAL WORLD

School of Business Administration Alumni Association
University of Minnesota

OCTOBER 2, 1962

THE title of this talk implies no intent to complain. I don't deplore the fact that we in business must live and work in a political world. On the contrary, we are lucky we can do so. We are lucky to be doing business in a country where political life is everyone's concern, and where public opinion, the public consensus, determines not only elections but the success or failure of every enterprise.

This is our democratic process. It is arduous and sometimes exasperating. However, this is what gives us in business our opportunities as well as our problems. And we ourselves are constantly furthering the process. How? By giving the public more and more choices. Every new breakfast food gives the kiddies something new to vote for. That is a facetious example, but I am only trying to suggest that the endless variety of industrial output, the visible and tangible results of enterprise, surely help to foster habits of judgment, of selection, of choice. There has never been a time when so many people could exercise, in the small affairs of everyday life, the option of yea or nay.

I would say too that a public so accustomed and educated is bound to demand from us in business the best we can deliver. I mean a quality job: good services, good products, good advertising, good value, good everything.

Moreover, the public verdict is not rendered in the market place alone. Some may think that the judgments people make in a drugstore or a used-car lot, or in a telephone booth, are unrelated to the judgments they arrive at in a voting booth. I don't think they are unrelated. Economic experience and political choice are mixed like Tom and Jerry. In our society the relations between industry and government do not begin in Washington. They begin in millions of minds that are influenced every day by the kind of job that we in business do: the goods we sell, the wages we pay, our behavior in the community, how we sound when we speak, and whether we show ourselves as people that other people can trust. And the mistakes we make, the shortcomings we exhibit, do not merely send customers into a competitor's arms. They also make people think as citizens, and influence their political decisions.

Quality performance, therefore, solid accomplishment, good citizenship—these are the necessary foundations for business progress in a political world. Perhaps this seems self-evident. I stress it however because I think we in business need to be sure of the ground we stand on before we raise our voices.

Great public decisions are in the making that will affect every aspect of business operations—taxes, employment, investment in the tools of progress, ability to compete in world markets. In all this decision making, it is vital that business be heard. Government needs to hear what we have to say; and I might add that I know few people in government who do not feel this need keenly. But lawmakers also know, and we must realize, that it is the caliber of our effort, our performance in action, that determines our competence to bear witness. If private enterprise were only a slogan, who would listen to the voice of business?

The success of Telstar® has told the world that government and industry in the United States can work together on the most complex problems. I think it tells too that in and out of the halls of Congress, inside and outside government, in newspaper offices and broadcasting stations, and in homes across the land, there is a deep underlying belief in our American system that only wants occasions for expression. There is a pride that wants to be nourished. There is a willingness for us in industry to show what we can do, and a strong desire to see us outdo ourselves. I have talked with senators who did not hesitate to say that when Telstar came through, their hearts beat a little faster. I have read editorials I wish I could have written myself. Let us not think that the spirit that made this country great is a thing of the past. Let us make it our business, rather, to pile up evidence to the contrary.

One of the most important decisions the country faces today is how the taxing power is to be applied in the years ahead. We have entered a new stage in economic history. We have passed through the time when world demand for nearly everything America could produce was so strong that the prevailing weight of taxation could still be successfully borne. We come now to a time when we must reshape, reorganize, re-equip ourselves to meet hard competition and keep our economy moving ahead. Some lightening of the tax burden is urgently needed; and if we in business feel this, if we are aware and alert to it, then we must be advocates. We will fail in our duty if we are not advocates. But we must also prove, in the purposes we enunciate and the actions we take, that private interest is not in conflict with public interest; rather, that the goals we set, and the means we use to achieve them, point toward progress for the nation as a whole.

I have spoken of taxation, important as it is, only as an example. The main point is that if we in American enterprise are as good as we say we are, and as right as we hope we are, we will not lack the brains and the public spirit to prove it. Or the patience, either. If you will bear with another reference to the Bell System, it took us nearly fifteen years after the war to get telephone charges in the various states on a basis that would compensate for the inroads of inflation and put us in a financial situation where our customers, employees, and share owners would not be subject to risks of inadequate service, diminished employment, or insufficient compensation, with every downward swing in the business cycle.

I can hardly think of a more distasteful task than making these upward changes in rates. But we did it because we felt it was the only right thing to do. Further, it was only accomplished because the regulatory authorities, no less than ourselves, faced the same facts, wrestled hard with them, and came to the conclusion that a better level of profit was important to progress. I think the results today clearly demonstrate how right they were. Because our financial situation is better, we can build for the future, maintain employment, and contribute much more, and more evenly, to the country's economic growth.

And I repeat, this is an accomplishment not of a business by itself, but of business and government working together. I don't mean it has all been sweetness and light, or ever will be. Things are never that way. Of course there are disagreements, and sometimes they are sharp. But we can and must build mutual respect and understanding.

To express one more thought about the business-government relationship, I believe the people who are actually in a business, and live with its problems every day, will make much better decisions than can ever be made by dictation from an outside source. Of course I don't say you should never take somebody else's advice. But our economy gets its vitality from the individual efforts of millions of people striving to solve their own problems. There is simply no substitute for this.

Incidentally, this is not to be understood as an objection to regulation of our kind of business. We know the need for that. But regulation is one thing and management is another, and I might add that most regulators I know are well aware of this.

I believe, finally, that if management is to say, "Let us do the managing," then it is our bounden duty to require and nourish competence in people all through our organizations. I said nourish as well as require because it isn't enough just to ask for it. You have to work at it all the time, in hiring and training, in judging and promoting, in challenging people and holding them accountable. This is the biggest task of any business large or small, and how well we do it will determine the future of all business in the United States.

I have tried in this talk to say that business must both perform and speak well; that ours is the great responsibility of nourishing and advancing the spirit and abilities of private enterprise; that the quality of our effort will not go unrecognized; that notwithstanding differences, industry and government can work together. In conclusion I will only say again, we can and must build mutual respect and understanding. This is the road, in our political world, toward business performance, and national performance, that everyone can be proud of.

BUSINESS PURPOSE AND PUBLIC OPINION

Chamber of Commerce of Greater Philadelphia

MARCH 20, 1963

As I have thought about the problems of business in the United States, it seems to me that one of the central needs we face is to establish what our driving purposes really are.

There are any number of people outside of business who are fluent in telling us what they think our purposes ought to be. But purposes can not be established from the outside in. They have to be shaped from the inside out.

I don't mean that public opinion has no influence. It has enormous influence, and we in business had better listen to it. But this influence is effective only as it helps you and me, all of us in our respective businesses, to think out for ourselves, and to our own conviction, good, sound, solid purposes that command respect and inspire hard effort.

To say it a little differently, public opinion will always have the last word. But what that last word will be depends on our shaping worthwhile goals, and putting on the kind of performance that is required to reach them.

I heard this point made the other day, that in the modern world the effort to create good "images" is replacing, to a considerable extent, the effort to reach ideals. I think this is so, and I wish it were not. How can a business exert a praiseworthy influence on its own people, let alone government and the general public, if all it is trying to do is create a good "corporate image"? An image of what, one may ask. It is only what we really are that in the long run will have impact—not our idea of how we ought to look in a rose-colored mirror.

I have heard myself quoted sometimes as saying that business and government can and must work together. There is nothing wrong with the quotation. However, I urgently want this to be, not on the basis that business works with government because it has no other choice, but on the basis that government works with business because that is the best choice it can conceivably make.

I am a private enterpriser from my hat to my socks. I also think, however, that there is no enterprise so private that it can do without public spirit.

Surely the economic growth we are all striving for depends first and foremost on the drive that is generated in the private sector of the economy.

Surely it depends on stimulating and rousing the energies of private enterprise.

Surely it depends on encouraging the acceptance of risk and the enthusiastic exercise of management skills.

Surely too (or so it seems to me) unless government tax and labor policies lead to a higher degree of profitability than is now realized by business as a whole, manipulation of the economy will not bring good and may bring great harm.

I feel these things strongly. Perhaps many of you do also. But at the same time, I am convinced that for the business I am in, our right to be heard, our success, our very existence, depend on producing public value that could not be produced in any other way. And this in turn requires, I am sure, purposes that while practical in character, still stand before us as ideals (not "images") that demand the best effort we can make.

I may feel, for example, that government proposals and programs are sometimes way off the mark with respect to providing incentives for business and encouraging economic progress. And when we in industry feel this way, it is vital that we say so and say why, not just express our opinions, but give the reasons that support our views.

But I do not think we can look to government to *give* private enterprise vitality. Government can never do this. It can only give us reasonable freedom to demonstrate what *we* can do. The initiative that businessmen themselves apply to their tasks, the goals they establish, the zeal they exercise, the demands they make on themselves to produce increasing public value, these are the major determinants of private enterprise in the United States.

To add just one more thought, when you commit yourself to the public plainly, you go out on a limb, you give hostages to performance that must be redeemed. I think more businesses are learning that by the very act of stating their purposes, and doing this in public, they greatly encourage their own effort to achieve them.

WHO PROFITS FROM RISK?

Los Angeles Rotary Club

JUNE 14, 1963

I GAVE this talk that title because I wanted to talk generally about the encouragement of risk taking. The main point I have in mind is that the benefits or profits from well-considered business risks are pervasive and flow in all directions.

Who profits from risk? Obviously not everyone all the time; ours is a profit and loss system, and the word "risk" means just what it says. But the successful risks bring profit not just to a business but to its customers, in fact to them first of all, for it is surely they who profit most when business is encouraged to venture and innovate, to open new roads, to offer new goods and services and create new orders of value.

Likewise, to create employment in this growing nation, with its rapidly increasing labor force, we simply must have profits that are sufficient to attract capital and spur investment to meet new needs.

But let me use another word here instead of "profits." The word I want is "profitability." And the distinction is important. It is a great mistake to measure prosperity in total profits as the country grows. It is downright misleading. The fact is, total profits can grow while profitability declines, in which case the employment problem, for example, is more aggravated than helped. It is profitability, nothing else, the ability to profit from risk, that is essential to create new investment that expands employment.

Profit for everyone—this is what our profit system, our private enterprise system, our private risk system, can and must accomplish. This, to me, is everlastingly the goal to shoot for. But it is a goal that can be realized only if the hope of profit for the enterpriser stirs his enthusiasm and impels him to accept the discipline of risk.

I said I wanted to talk about this generally and I do. But I can't ignore the time and place I am in. Here in California, as it happens, the profitability of the Bell System has been limited to a level that I would have to call marginal at best. I believe this would have a depressing and deadening effect if it should prevail across the country.

I won't take your time with this at length, but will only make a few points briefly. If Bell System earnings generally were limited as they are in this state, in my judgment we could not obtain on sound terms all the capital we need. We would be forced to go slow on new construction to introduce improvements. We would not have the same confidence and active interest on the part of more than two million share owners. We could hardly carry on a research and development program of the same depth and breadth as that in which we are currently engaged. I don't see how we could avoid trimming back some of the tremendous investment we are making each year not only to meet and anticipate growth, but also to modernize communication equipment and introduce new and improved services for business, for agriculture, for government, and for the home. In short, I would say the almost certain results would be less construction, less service improvement, less progress, less employment, and a lesser tax contribution to help meet the needs of local, state, and federal government.

Now I shall leave such disturbing comment and get to a more cheerful note.

It seems to me that around the country there *is* coming to be a better understanding of the function of business profit than I could sense a few years ago. I haven't any attitude surveys to prove it, but I think there are indicators. It also seems to me that some of the strongest come straight from Washington. For all the differences of viewpoint among businessmen on policies and programs (and there are certainly wide differences) nevertheless I sense that increasingly, leaders in government do recognize the need for vitality in the private sector of the economy; they do understand that the dynamo of profit is essential for economic growth; they do know that financial strength in your business and mine is the necessary foundation on which to build the future.

I have to say also, however, that I wish I could see this point of view in clear language and bold type in the economic textbooks. Teaching economics without centering attention on risk and profit is like making a watch without the works. The hands will not move. Nor will the young people in this country be able to tell the time of day in an economic sense.

Another aspect of profiting from risk is the effect of risk on individual people and hence on the character of the business they are working in. I am quite sure the managers in any business need the experience of running risks more or less constantly and learning the consequences whether they are good or bad, welcome or unwelcome. They have to find out that a good risk and good judgment on it will bring reward, and a poor risk its penalty. Otherwise I don't see how they will develop the personal qualities that produce a quality job.

What any business needs is the urge to do its damnedest, and this takes people who have that urge. I don't see financial reward as the only source of it. There are other factors that are equally important, and for many people, much more so. But we need all sources of energy and drive, not just some of them. I am simply saying that the opportunity for healthy profit, the knowledge that real ability and top performance will have their reward—these are vital to developing the discipline, the alertness, and the judgment that people must have to make a great business.

If I were to single out the one thing in our business that might be called most important to our future, I would say it is the spirit in individual managers that makes them alive and sensitive to every opportunity to get something done tomorrow just a little better than they see it being done today. And this same spirit will have to operate inside them to build the personal competence they need, because nobody can fix anything if he doesn't know how. It isn't just a matter of applying old experience, it is a matter of being dedicated to get new experience too. This kind of dedication isn't generated in a static atmosphere. A stodgy boss can discourage it. The weight of the rule book can press it down. Finicky regulation can put a dead-end sign in front of it. Taxation that walks off with the fruits of effort can kill it. Public distrust, a general political or public view that business needs to be held down, confined, supervised, restrained, limited, curbed, controlled—these are bound to weaken the will of individuals to dedicate their best to business life.

I am going to say again however that I think public understanding of the importance of lively, vital, successful private enterprise is growing. I think more people are realizing that profit is the prime mover of economic progress, the engine that creates new investment, new productive wealth, and new jobs for a rapidly growing labor force. I think it is more and more widely understood that *without* adequate margins of profit in the private sector of the economy, the country can never attain a more favorable rate of economic growth. Just as an indication of this understanding, let me remind you that with all the uncertainties that surround federal tax policy and legislation, there seems to be no disagreement today on the fundamental goal of increasing business activity *and* profit that will ultimately yield increased total tax revenues.

If I am right in this, then it seems to me it emphasizes all over again what a tremendous responsibility we in business have.

We have the responsibility to produce public value that could not be produced in any other way.

We have the responsibility to set goals for ourselves that we will have to strain to reach.

We have the responsibility to speak out on existing or proposed policies that may interfere with our doing our best—I don't mean just stating opinions, but giving the facts and the reasons behind our views.

We have the responsibility to give employees challenge to grow on, and to build managers who can do everything tomorrow better than you and I can do it today.

We have the responsibility to increase day-to-day efficiency and equally to make the most intelligent use of profit and all capital funds.

We have the responsibility to discern consumer wants more acutely, and to meet them more promptly and with greater imagination.

We have the responsibility for constant research and innovation.

We have the responsibility to live by ethical standards that will operate to improve every aspect of our job.

You may say this all sounds idealistic but I say we had better be idealistic and no mistake about it. There is no conflict between being realistic and being idealistic. There is no conflict between working hard for fair rewards and being fair in business dealings. No one can always be right, but he can always try.

Can free enterprise serve private aims *and* public ends? I not only believe it can, I am sure it must.

So far as the Bell System is concerned, we think our job, our mission, is to put communication services at your disposal that will exceed your best expectations. In widening the range of these services, I will just say in conclusion, we have imparted to our own business a considerably higher degree of risk than we faced in the past. Optional features, conveniences, and arrangements of one sort or another all introduce new elements of risk. But we have acted with our eyes open. We hope regulatory commissions will be progressive and objective enough to see the public value in a rate of profitability that is consistent with these risks. And we have the strong hope and determination, likewise, that the answer to the question, "Who profits from *our* risk?" will be, in one word—everyone.

Science and Engineering

THREE-DIMENSIONAL ENGINEERS

American Institute of Electrical Engineers

NEW YORK, JANUARY 21, 1957

IN this dynamic and expanding world the competent engineer has to lead a dynamic and expanding life. There is no room left for routine approaches to engineering, or for standing still with the mental equipment we've got. The engineer has to grow and change with the times, and constantly equip himself to handle new problems. He has to nourish his mind and broaden his outlook to make sure that neither gets obsolete. And at all times, he has to look ahead.

We need the most in creative imagination, ability to take on new assignments, and selective judgment. I think the growing tendency in the schools to concentrate on fundamentals is very helpful to this, because the first need is to develop the basic mental equipment. There remains to industry the great responsibility to provide not only first-rate technical training but also to make sure the able engineer never gets locked in his technical closet.

To be sure, he always remains an engineer, with a sound grasp of engineering fundamentals that never grow obsolete. But he also becomes something more. As he applies ever changing arts he is also thoughtful of their effects. He gains and uses knowledge of marketing and finance. He interprets between designer and salesman. He perceives and understands the general wants and particular problems of other people, whether he holds a supervisory position or not.

I think our need in the Bell System for engineers of ability and imagination is typical. We need them like grass needs rain. And I think we can make rain.

We won't do it by just tagging or labeling people as engineers. We won't do it by putting engineers into compartments and shutting them off from the rest of the ship. We won't do it by cramming size forty-two men into size thirty-six jobs, or vice versa. We won't do it by setting so-called minimum standards and then sitting back and letting nature take its course.

We *will* do it I believe through intelligent and concerted effort to develop what I call three-dimensional engineers.

The first dimension we'll say is what you got in college, that showed you how to move in a straight line in your first particular field.

The second dimension is in continued training and self-study, that broadens a person and keeps him up-to-date with technological changes so he can solve problems in broad areas and new areas of engineering.

The third dimension is the height that comes from the mixing and mingling of engineering and management ideas, so that the engineer's understanding of the problems and requirements *of* the business makes him more effective *in* the business. This understanding comes not only from study but from shoulder-to-shoulder association and contact and interaction between engineering, operating, financial, and merchandising people. And we need this third dimension not here and there among engineers but everywhere, so they will have a volume effect on the business. If engineering is to be solid, it has to have this volume.

BUSINESS NEEDS BASIC RESEARCH

The Economic Club of New York

JANUARY 21, 1958

TODAY all industry in the free world faces a new kind of competition. Soviet science has stepped out into space ahead of us, and it would be sheer folly not to recognize its driving will to step ahead in every other way. This is not just a matter of missiles and satellites. It is much, much more. It is a matter of markets, of leadership in trade and commerce, of the power of free industry to strengthen the public welfare and to win and keep worldwide esteem.

In the past American industry has led the world largely because we have used existing knowledge with great ingenuity, developed new products, and introduced all kinds of innovations in organizing people and machines.

But now, as I have said, we face the new and mighty competition of science and new knowledge in the hands of determined men who have flatly told us they mean to rule the world.

Can competition on this plane be successfully countered by purely industrial and productive skills alone? Not in my judgment: no more than the competition of the telephone could be met by the most artful ingenuity in the development, design, and mass production of megaphones; no more than the internal combustion engine could be matched by giving the horse an extra quart of oats and putting ball bearings on the buggy.

It seems clear that the country as a whole is waking up to the need for science that will bring new knowledge in abundance. And we are getting more of it, much more, than we were getting twenty or even ten years ago. The part I want to touch on is only the part of industry. Is the quest for knowledge something that really belongs in industry? Or does it belong rather in the universities and in government, with industry applying the results?

Certainly basic research must be done by the universities and government, but I believe there is great advantage, and great need, to do it within industry as well. For this there are several reasons.

The first is that the interaction of basic research with the other phases of an industry stimulates everybody. Basic researchers and development engineers working fairly close to each other in a dynamic atmosphere sharpen each others' wits. Why then should an industry choose to do without this stimulus, in fact, how can it afford to do without it?

A second reason is that the technical organization which includes a basic research group thereby takes out insurance against possible costly mistakes. The cost of development is far greater than the cost of research, and if a big undertaking gets off on the wrong foot the price is terribly high. Granting that any careful organization will try to guard against this, still there is no precaution quite as sound and sure as having basic research people right in the organization who are working at the deepest roots of the problem.

A third reason is that at any particular time, university scientists may not be working on the things that would do your business the most good. No matter how important their work is to them or to others, it may not be getting the new knowledge that *you* most need. A good example is the work which produced the transistor. University physicists were busy on other things. Our Bell System research opened up the field.

Research Costs

The cost of research is obviously a risk. But in any field of business, if we face new problems we must take new action. If we face new danger we must take new chances. And if the danger we face is to fall behind in knowledge, then it seems to me that taking the new risk becomes imperative.

Moreover, while we shouldn't underestimate the cost, we

shouldn't overestimate it either. The fact is that a large business can do a lot through expenditures which, in relation to total volume, ought not to frighten anybody.

Someone may say, "That is all very well, but you in the Bell System have a pretty stable business and you don't have to meet the same kind of competition that other businesses do." The fact is that we work under regulation and on a lower profit margin than most big industry. We do basic research on a thrift basis and we get back far more than we put in. Others who have ample resources would in my opinion get back at least as much as we do.

I think most of the hesitation about going into basic research is due to a worry that all the money may go down the drain. However, when you put the cost into perspective with everything else a big business does, I don't, as I've said, see much cause for alarm. Finally, if you will accept the proposition that we have a new kind of competition to meet, and must have new knowledge to meet it, then I think it ought not to be hard to show the stockholders that knowledge-building dollars are a good risk against the ultimate calamity of having commissars run your business.

Requirements for Successful Research

Now I shall summarize some of the principles we regard as necessary to the success of basic research in the Bell System.

The first is to get the best possible people. Getting new knowledge takes a special brand of brains. And they must be well and deeply trained. Without this combination, nothing will be accomplished.

Second, you have to have an objective but you also have to give the brains full freedom. Maybe those two things will strike you as mutually exclusive. That hasn't been our experience. We have the broad objective of improving electrical communication. This is a perfectly clear goal. At the same time it gives the research scientist full scope for the exercise of his creative power. If you question this, I suggest you ask our scientists.

What is meant by freedom for the researcher?

He must be free to do what he wants to do, in keeping with

the broad objective, and knows he can do best. If a line of work is proposed and he says "no," take his word for it. He knows more than you do.

The scientist must also be free to plan his work in his own way. You cannot plan it for him. This means there are no schedules. There is no program by the clock or even by the calendar.

The research scientist should also be free to publish his findings without undue delay. And you should also let him carry his work up to the point where he is sure its meaning is fully grasped by those who will go on with the development.

The third and most difficult essential in maintaining basic research is to keep the researcher from becoming a developer. This is the mistake that every research scientist will warn the business manager against. When basic research is swallowed up by development, then basic research stops. The only assurance of getting new knowledge is to insist that the research group stay a research group. When one piece of research is done, the results must be given to others for development and the researchers must turn to a new basic problem.

Finally, basic research today needs adequate equipment. For example, in our Bell Laboratories research we study the basic characteristics of all kinds of materials. To do this we must look at them in every possible way. This requires using many different tools, and they represent a not inconsiderable investment.

Another thing I ought to emphasize is the disposition and temper of the manager who holds the purse strings. Of course he is itching for results. But he will have to be patient. Whenever I get impatient, there are two thoughts I use to restrain myself. The first is that research requires no more patience on my part than it does of the man who is doing the work. And the second thought that helps me is, thank heaven we have the research that I can be impatient about.

Does Business Have a Responsibility for Research?

For many years now big business has been under the necessity of justifying its existence. This is perfectly natural. Big business *does* affect the lives of everyone and it *must* continuously prove by its actions that everyone benefits. To me, and I daresay to you, the evidence of the benefits is overwhelming:

In the capacity to take on big jobs that depend on big investment.

In the creation of new opportunities for small business.

In the sheer ability to produce in vast quantity at low price.

In the strength that armed ourselves and our allies in two world wars, and but for which this country today might be an overseas province of, let us say, the Third Reich.

Our need to prove ourselves will never end, but I want to make this observation: It seems to me that at no time in this century has the man in the street had more reason or instinct to look hopefully and even prayerfully to big business than he has right now. He has a thunderclap awareness that it is big and mighty effort which has rocketed a living creature up out of the atmosphere and into the silence of space. His instinct and acknowledgment *must* be that the Soviets' kind of bigness can only be countered by another kind of bigness, and I mean our kind, which mixes bigness and freedom. So I think today we have the *potential* for a new degree of public understanding of big business, and a new public awareness that the future depends very largely on big industry and on keeping it sound and strong.

To say this, however, is only to say that our responsibility grows accordingly. If industry should fall short, not in skill or ingenuity, or organizational teamwork, or productive or marketing savvy, not in any of these things, *but in getting new knowledge,* then what degree of public understanding and approval should we expect, say, ten or twenty years from now? And is that the kind of risk we want to take?

Freedom Is Needed to Meet the Responsibility

Finally, let me address a few remarks to those people both in and out of public office who for reasons best known to themselves seem dedicated to the effort to harass and attack big business, and to cut it down to some other size of their own choosing.

I ask them to stop, look, and listen. A few minutes ago I was saying that the cost of basic research is nothing for a big business to be scared of. However, I didn't say it was free. It is in fact big enough to require big resources. For one thing, the research group needs to be large enough for its members to spark each other, and to attract the topnotch people who want to work in a scientific community that draws others of equal caliber.

So if basic research within industry is really going to grow, it is going to have to grow in big organizations. I don't mean there isn't room for it in smaller ones, especially when they are doing work for the government and the cost gets paid that way. But if industry as a whole is going to get up a full head of steam in acquiring new knowledge, the impetus has got to come from big business which has the means to pay for it.

How can those who continually attack big business expect us to accept this new kind of risk if they keep us forever preoccupied with the effort to keep ourselves whole? This is simply not the way to get on with the vital tasks that we must get on with.

So I say sincerely and urgently to those in public life: By all means, hold us in big business to our responsibilities. But give us, also, the freedom to build the strength that we need to meet them.

THE USE OF TECHNICAL RESOURCES

Massachusetts Institute of Technology Second Century Fund Dinner

NEW YORK, MAY 7, 1963

ONE thing that bothers many thoughtful people (inside the universities as well as outside) is the effect of all this federal money now flowing to the schools, especially for science and technology. The worrisome thing is that if a disproportionate amount of money and talent are expended for a few purposes, not enough work can be done on other things that are tremendously important too. The same kind of problem exists in many businesses, including the one I am in. We are always having to decide what jobs should come ahead of others.

I am not suggesting that the country today can make the kind of scientific and economic progress it needs without large sums of government money going to the schools for research. I am simply saying that the allocation of all time, money, and effort is a matter of crucial importance.

Regarding this, our friends at M.I.T. have pointed out that funds from non-government sources are all the more needed to maintain a balance in support of the independence of the schools.

I don't disagree with this, but I doubt that even millions of dollars of private support will be enough *by themselves* to establish a balance. All that private money can do in this situation is to strengthen the will of the educators to manage their total assignment wisely.

To be specific, there are at least two parties to every federal grant of funds. One is the grantor and the other is the grantee. What this means is that the worth of every project is open to critical evaluation and judgment at both ends of the line. And it needs, it must have, the benefit of both judgments. Especially, those who are invited to undertake research and development work must be able to feel that each project lies in an area where their talents are genuinely needed and can be employed to important advantage.

There is no question that the people who grant government funds have an enormous responsibility. But the responsibility of those who are invited to accept them is at least equal, and I would say even greater, for no one else can judge as well as they can whether a proposition will result in the best possible use of somebody else's money and their own effort and time.

Here we have in our modern society these magnificent resources in science and technology, resources of a kind never before available in the whole history of mankind. I can think of nothing more important than that they be applied to the full limit of their potential value. These resources are precious. We cannot afford to see any of them wasted, either in industry or in the universities. We cannot afford to see them misapplied. And their most fruitful application, I am convinced, will come only through the exercise of calm, independent judgment by people and institutions that are not thrown off balance by streams of dollars, some of which might just possibly be flowing in the wrong direction.

So I hope this institution, refreshed and strengthened by the outpouring of funds from private resources, will more than ever set an example of firm good judgment—will more than ever help and inspire others in both university and industrial laboratories to ask the questions that lead toward right answers.

I have a few other hopes that I shall mention briefly.

I think the most valuable thing any school can do for a student is to help him get set on a course of continuous personal growth (assuming, naturally, that he has some potential). How to learn and keep on learning, this is what counts. For the scientist or engineer especially, it is not a merely desirable attribute, it is a necessity. Science *is* learning. That is its essence. And its application in new arts, new systems, new products and services, this equally demands the drive and determination to learn.

It has been said a thousand times that the pace of modern technology is so fast that the education of the engineer must be continuous. This is true enough. But I think you can also turn it around and say it another way: If the drive to learn is not continuous, then the pace of technology will be neither so fast nor so productive.

Another point about education in science and engineering has been often expressed, but I can't help saying it again. I recall reading somewhere that Faraday declined to be described as a physicist. He didn't want to be classified in purely technical terms. He didn't care to be tagged as perhaps not wanting other endowments as well. He desired breadth of learning, and of being, and of understanding, as well as depth. And it seems to me that for the modern scientist or engineer, the person who is building the tools that will change the world, this is more important than ever. He will have to keep growing just to keep up with the techniques of his profession, and hopefully, to advance them. But there is more besides, for his responsibility is not alone technical, it is human and moral.

Dr. Fisk, president of Bell Laboratories, made a little talk the other day to a group of students. I was much interested to see the emphasis he put on various responsibilities that rest with engineers, the responsibility for communicating as well as for doing; the responsibility for working in tune with other people, and, often, for organizing and leading their co-operative effort; the responsibility for discerning what *ought* to be done as well as for knowing how to do it; the responsibility for professional accomplishment that reflects good understanding of human experience and human aspiration.

In the business I am in we mix solid-state physics, corporate finance, and day-by-day effort to meet the needs and wishes of millions of people, no two of whom are exactly alike. That is an oversimplified way to put it, but the point is that the technical and the economic and the human are not separate, they touch each other all along the line. And the people who have undergone scientific and engineering disciplines are involved not partially, but all the way. They are involved in the economic, social, and political circumstances to which their work contributes. They are involved in the problems they create as well as in the problems they solve. They are intimately involved in the processes of decision, and they need the breadth of outlook, the awareness of alternatives, the insight into possible consequences, that good decisions require. The man of brilliant technical attainments can ill afford to appear as an amateur outside of his special field.

I do not want to see M.I.T. turn out this, that, or the other type or types of men. The need of the world is not for types, it is for individuals, each with his own integrity and his own desire to give the best he can make of himself to something outside himself. I see a lot of what passes for scientific and engineering activity going on these days that somehow seems to lack the ring of silver. Maybe a contract tempts a group or an individual into short cuts. Maybe expediency dictates answers. Maybe jobs are being attempted by people not qualified to attempt them. Maybe things are being done that ought not to be done at all. This is just an impression I have and I decline to particularize. But I do have the impression and it makes me want to say to the people at M.I.T. and every institution in the land where the heritage of science and engineering is nurtured—send us, I beseech you, men who are scrupulous of their talents, who feel that something important has been entrusted to them, who prize their responsibility, who insist on themselves and will not let themselves down.

BUSINESS AND SCIENCE

International Management Congress

NEW YORK, SEPTEMBER 16, 1963

FOR many years the Bell System has endeavored to bring management, science, and technology closely together. This experience persuades us that successful conduct of a science-based enterprise depends on continuous consultation among the people responsible for managerial, scientific, and engineering aspects of the business. The responsibility for decision rests with the head of the business, but the decision itself is the product of multiple judgments. And these judgments are themselves resultants. They result from the impact of the market on the laboratory, and from the potential influence of scientific discovery on the market. They reflect the interaction of public need, the state of our technical resources, and the economics of the business.

All of which means that marketer, manager, engineer, and scientist must each be able to understand what the others are saying, and to make himself understood. Also, each must have a proper sense of the limits of his own expertise; there must be a mutual recognition of strengths and individual acknowledgment of limitations.

In our business we want this relationship between managerial and technical associates to inspire diverse talents in co-ordinated effort. We want it to be satisfying to very different minds. And we want it to produce good economic and social results.

To accomplish these purposes, in our thinking two things are essential.

Clear Goals

First, a business needs goals that are clear and that have wide range and reach. Aims must be explicitly stated, and they must be of a quality that challenges superior minds.

In the Bell System our continuous purpose has been to find and use every resource that will contribute to the advancement of communications. The scientist's prime interest may be in the finding, and the engineer's or manager's in the using. But in all of us, this broad purpose exerts a strong and steady pull. It helps us to know what we are doing and why.

The Systems Approach

The second essential is also the key to the first. We believe the successful union of business and science depends fundamentally on systems thinking, the systems approach, the concept that underlies systems engineering.

I suppose our particular experience brought us earlier to this conclusion than has been the case in numerous other industries. The telephone network is so clearly and obviously a system. No single element is of value by itself. It is only when all elements, millions and even billions of them, are conjoined in the system and function satisfactorily, that the usefulness of each is revealed and the system as a whole is of value.

But in what kind of system, representing what choices? And what is the map of the system, what are its boundaries? Where do the roads lead, of what stone shall they be made, and for what kind of traffic by how many people for how many years? And at what cost? Or to sum up many of these words in another that we can't seem to get along without these days, what are the parameters?

The essence of the systems approach as we see it is to get, first, a clear view of what is both needed and potentially feasible; second, a closely reasoned determination of the best course for achieving the desired result; and third, a dependable measure of the means already available, and those we must still discover, in order to make doable what we are setting out to do.

A Common Language

I have said that the marketer, manager, scientist, and engineer must be able to talk and listen to each other. But for this they need a common language.

In our experience a common language is considerably advanced by the systems concept, which aims to bring together all relevant considerations of need, probable use, alternative methods and structures, available resources, and problems still to be solved.

Perhaps to some of you the term "systems engineering" has a purely technical ring; and I agree that in the narrow sense it describes specific technical and scientific studies. How then can systems thinking help to build a common language?

To understand how, we need only remember the principles on which systems engineering is based:

To appraise need and feasibility.

To evaluate alternatives.

To distinguish between what is known and not known.

To do all this to the end that the most efficient, practical, and useful system can be created.

I would say that these principles are not narrow but are very broad indeed. They have meaning to marketer, manager, engineer, and scientist alike. And in any endeavor, when the undertaking is seen by all as involving systems principles, a common language is bound to be encouraged. To say it another way, the systems concept *demands* that people understand each other, all the way from the salesman who must learn the customer's problems and wants, to the engineers and scientists who know what we can do today and are constantly probing the possibilities of tomorrow.

Systems Thinking Clarifies Goals

I said also that a business must have clear goals meaningfully expressed. In our belief the systems approach is essential to reveal goals and test their validity. What shall we do, and why and how and when?—it is all these questions, not just some of them, and how they are all to be answered, that give a business the fullest measure of useful purpose.

I might observe too that getting a clear idea of what is doable does not reduce research and development to pedestrian or unimaginative courses. Looking before you leap need not shorten the length of the jump, but it does help you prepare for it, and it can sometimes tell you, also, whether there is anything on the other side. What cannot be afforded is to squander talent, time, and money on haphazard undertakings, dreamy projects that have little chance of bearing fruit, or ventures that will be proved idle by the course of events.

You will not infer, I am sure, that efforts in basic research are limited to filling gaps in knowledge indicated by systems studies. This is far from being the case. In our own business, we wish to explore all fields of knowledge that hold promise of increasing our competence in the communications art. The charter of the research scientist is wide indeed. Yet he needs to know, like everyone else in the business, what business he is in, and the relevance of his part to the whole. And the systems concept might be said to steady the general direction of our research effort, by helping us to understand better what our business really is.

The Orderly Application of Research

In our judgment, the systems approach is essential to any expectation that the application of scientific research in industry will be orderly and that useful purposes will be most effectively served. And I do not mean just in the communications industry. We are obviously a system, as I said, and the exigencies of our business forced this thinking on us long ago, as it did on certain other industries as well. For still others, my belief is that the future will demand it—and for some this may even be a matter of survival. Just to reinforce that thought a little, in recent years one of the fashionable methods for attempting to insure survival has been diversification; but in some cases, as one watches companies that have marched off in all directions go through the stressful experience of marching back again, one wonders whether a little more system and a little less diversity might not have been more fruitful.

Knowledge and Guesswork

I venture to say that no business has more consistently sought new knowledge than the Bell System, or has been on the whole more successful in producing and using it. And the results have been of great value not only to ourselves, but in seeding progress in other industries. Yet with all this, I would still say that the prime need in modern technology is for wiser, smarter thought and action about what we have, rather than reliance on a headlong hunt for miracle solutions, or brute-force, extravagant effort to find what we do not have. I would still say that the most significant impact of science on our technical systems will come from better methods for studying and laying out what choices really exist, and for differentiating between what we know and what we can merely guess.

How we handle information is critically important. The systems concept relies essentially on information handling, and now in high-speed computers we have new tools to help us employ the concept more effectively than ever before. The effects of different elements in the situation can be evaluated. The future performance of systems can be simulated. Their economic and social effectiveness can be estimated more accurately. I don't say that management intuition can be dispensed with. I don't believe it ever can be. But intuition never suffers from having facts to work on, and my point is simply that today's tools give the systems concept new dimensions.

The Discipline of Free Markets

The next thought that I have expresses a deep personal belief. I think the free market system is the best hope for proper selective use of science and technology in the public interest. Competition for public favor, in my judgment, is the single most important factor in making the results of research of greatest use to the greatest number. The forces of the market powerfully demand that technology keep in touch with human needs and produce what people deem of value. They likewise subject technical effort to the harsh discipline of profit and loss, a discipline that has no patience with the fantastic and is always at war with waste. In the fire of this discipline competitive technology creates the services, the products, the improvements and options, that people are willing to pay for and provide profits to industry withal.

Before I conclude, I would like to comment briefly about scrupulousness, about integrity. The disciplines of science and engineering are rigorous. They have to be. Otherwise nothing of value is accomplished. The orderly application of scientific research to useful purposes depends on quality minds. In the creation of a technical system, when all factors are evaluated, including those of time and cost, compromises are inevitable. But the proper purpose of such compromise is to effect a combination of resources, a total system, that will best suit the purpose it is intended for. This is compromise in the interest of integrity, so to speak. No other kind is permissible. If a business allows itself to be pressured into merely expedient practice, and technical people of fine ability and conscience are asked to cut cloth accordingly, two results will ensue. First, the technical system that the business started out to create will be punched full of holes; and second, the quality minds will go somewhere else. However else the fortunes of the business may develop, it will not succeed in the scientific way. A form of Gresham's law will operate, and the good men will find other places to do what they are intent on doing. Similarly, able scientists will not feel at home in a business atmosphere where claims overstate accomplishments and talking outruns doing.

In conclusion let me accent once more that the orderly application of scientific research to useful purposes, by industry, requires that the scientific revolution be assimilated in the evolution of industrial enterprise. For this to be accomplished, the goals of research must be consistent with business goals and these goals must be clear and meaningful to scientists, managers, and engineers alike. In the systems concept, science itself has given us a means for distinguishing significant goals and a framework for mutual understanding among technical and managerial people.

This concept is cleanly functional. It insists on a sharp view of what is needed and can be done. It demands that information be organized so that all aspects of a problem may be known as exactly as possible, and all the resources needed to meet it. It isolates areas in which more knowledge is needed for valid purposes, and thereby adds meaning to basic research without interfering in the slightest with the freedom of research effort. It emphasizes step-by-step progress, and discourages the squandering of talent in extravagant pursuit of miracle solutions. Finally, it affords, not complete assurance, but a reasonable basis for prejudging the economic and social effectiveness of future technical systems.

National Defense

COMMUNICATIONS FOR DEFENSE

New York Chamber of Commerce

JANUARY 6, 1959

Two words, speed and control, describe the essence of a modern communication system. Anyone who uses the telephone is aware of the speed. However the control factor is just as important. For instance, the electrical path you talk over must be precisely controlled throughout its whole length. Also, the right path must be selected out of countless possibilities, and this too is control.

Speed and control are also essential in warfare. They always have been. Military people use words like mobility and command but the meaning is the same. Command is control and this is clearly a matter of communication. Today also we know the speed *of* control is vital, that is, command must be exercised almost instantly over vast distances. Hence the arts of communication are called on to the limit.

The Need for Dependability

In considering dependability, let's look first at the overall telephone network, because this is of basic importance. The network is enormous, and every last inch can be linked together. Moreover, the intercity lines are diversified so that we have more than one route between principal cities and very often several. We also have alternate routes around cities. All of this is to help protect the communication system so that we can handle emergency messages under any circumstances. With this in mind, in recent years we have built thousands of miles of cross-country lines that do not traverse critical target areas but skirt by them at a good distance. One such "express" route goes all the way from Maine to California. In other cases we have built communication arcs or circles around big cities. These connect with already existing routes in outlying areas. As a result calls can be made between any two major cities in the country without going through any of the most critical target areas.

This diversity, the great size of the total network, and its complete interconnection, are the nation's prime assets to insure uninterrupted communication—control—command. The reason is not hard to understand. If any control system, civil or military, depends on a single communication facility which is separate from all the rest, then its destruction leaves no option. The communications it was intended to provide are gone, period. What is essential is that facilities be integrated, so that if one part is lost another can be used.

The second essential is the operating know-how of hundreds of thousands of telephone people. Like the facilities they build and operate, they too are spread all over the map, and their skill and devotion are always "at the ready" to keep the service going.

Special Networks

Within the big total network are numerous special networks serving military and other defense agencies. These cover hundreds of thousands of miles of route and their circuit mileage is in the millions.

Some are voice networks, some are teletypewriter, still others carry complex data from outlying radar stations. Some converge on NORAD, or North American Air Defense headquarters in Colorado. Other networks radiate from Strategic Air Command headquarters near Omaha. These reach SAC air bases throughout the country, with connections to others overseas. Still another network is ready twenty-four hours a day to spread general warning to the nation. In all these operations, the need for dependability is paramount.

Seagoing telephone cables are another important aspect of our defense job. These are among the most sophisticated developments in the whole art of communications. I hope you will not overlook how important they are to defense. They are not subject to interruption by magnetic storms. They cannot be "jammed." They have greater capabilities than overseas radiotelephone circuits, and are more dependable.

Construction of the DEW Line

The Bell System was asked in December, 1954, to engineer and manage construction of the Distant Early Warning Line of radar stations in the Arctic. We delivered it thirty-two months later on schedule, fully tested, and ready to do its job.

To build the DEW Line men in ski planes landed where men had never been before, and shoveled landing strips for bigger planes which brought small tractors, which in turn cleared bigger strips for planes that could bring heavy tractors. Western Electric engineers devised new modes of construction to house men and equipment, supply water, store fuel, ventilate buildings, and protect against wind and fire. Bell Laboratories people, working with their fellow scientists at the Lincoln Laboratory, developed new techniques to insure reliable radar operation and dependable communication backward from the radar line. American and Canadian construction companies organized construction teams of thousands of men. All branches of the armed forces worked together to load and haul 460,000 tons of materials into the Arctic by ship, plane, and tractor train. Western Electric and telephone company technicians installed and tested equipment. Eskimos built igloos around aircraft in need of repair. Frogmen slipped into the water to blow up ice in the way of their ships. Going over the mountains some pilots died, and some of their passengers.

The human story of the DEW Line moves me every time I think of it. The same goes for the new Alaskan communication system known by the code name "White Alice." This covers thousands of miles across some of the most rugged country in the world. From the point farthest west, on a clear day you can see Siberia about fifty miles away. We designed, engineered, and installed White Alice (again with the help of many others) and turned it over to the military last March.

I sometimes hear people say offhand that projects like this are already out of date because they do not protect us from ballistic missiles. It doesn't seem to me that such comments are very thoughtful. Whatever the state of Russian progress on missiles, they also have thousands of manned aircraft. The less vulnerable we are to aircraft, the more difficult their military problem, the more time they need to solve it, and the more time we have to make ourselves more strong.

Important Requirements

Some of our habits of work in the Bell System have considerable bearing on why we have been asked to do certain military jobs.

For instance, in developing and manufacturing telephone equipment, our goal has always been to get the most reliable and economical *use,* not to sell the most articles in the fastest time. This emphasis on dependability fits right in with military needs. To illustrate: any electronic system you put in a missile, a few feet away from a screaming rocket engine, has to be rugged.

Again, Bell System people are accustomed to bringing a lot of things together to form complex systems. Any dial system, for example, is fairly complex. Long distance dialing is remarkably so. Experience of this sort is useful in creating military warning and weapon systems, which are very complex indeed.

Third, the Bell System integrates in one organization the functions of research, development, design, manufacture, and operation. Nowadays the people who have to develop and build weapon systems, and see to it that they work the way they are supposed to, are constantly knocking on the research man's door. They are always looking for new knowledge. They also need sure and certain knowledge about the materials they use. As one of our scientists puts it, "Weaponry today pushes things to the absolute limit so that only basic science can tell you when you are right."

All these factors have had much to do with our assignments on the Distant Early Warning Line, the SAGE air defense system (the term is short for Semi-Automatic Ground Environment), and Nike defensive missile systems.

We are also providing communications for what is called

BMEWS. That is the short name for a Ballistic Missile Early Warning System being developed for the Air Force. This is another project that reaches to the far North. It calls for handling data over long distances at very high speed as well as with complete reliability.

Some time ago Bell Laboratories designed and Western Electric built a 1,370-mile ocean cable from Cape Canaveral to Puerto Rico. This serves what is now known as the Atlantic Missile Range. The cable goes from island to island in the West Indies. Radar stations on the islands are connected to it, and the cable transmits data on missile test flights back to Canaveral.

Back in 1949 the Government asked us to manage the Atomic Energy Commission's Sandia Laboratory in New Mexico. This we have done for more than nine years. I doubt that many people have much notion of what an undertaking it is.

Sandia's job, in fewest words, is to design weapons around the nuclear explosive systems developed at other AEC laboratories, and then follow through on their production and reliability. Sandia develops fusing and firing systems, and the shape and structure of weapon casings. It does pilot manufacture and arranges for production by others. It is responsible for quality assurance. It designs handling equipment for weapon assembly and testing. It keeps watch over the stockpile to insure continuous reliability. It works out operating procedures and training manuals for the military.

Notice that the problems involved cover the whole spectrum of research, development, production, and operation. This in a nutshell is why we were asked to manage Sandia—because our organization, as I said, integrates experience in all these fields and the Government felt that this was what Sandia needed.

The Influence of Communications Research

Not much more than ten years ago three Bell Laboratories scientists—Brattain, Bardeen, and Shockley—invented the transistor. At about the same time Claude Shannon of the Laboratories reasoned out through mathematical analysis what has come to be known as "information theory" or "communication theory"—a fundamental conception that makes it possible to measure the efficiency of any communication system. It isn't to blow the Bell System's horn that I refer to these discoveries, though I am glad again to pay tribute to the men who made them. The important thing is that they are bound to have decisive influence on the whole future of communications, including military weapons and systems of command.

This is already happening. All guidance systems for ICBMs, for example, use transistorized computers. In fact, nearly all new military computers are being designed around transistors and related devices. A computer called TRADIC, developed at our Laboratories, pointed the way, and successors for many different military purposes are now under development in at least ten different industrial laboratories. Transistors function in the communication equipment that ties Nike batteries together. They convert radar signals into data. They are used in a system for the Navy which permits an aircraft carrier to direct the operations of a hundred different planes simultaneously over a single radio channel. They send word back to earth from our satellites in space.

I could give other examples but these are enough for now. I only want to suggest that out of basic research in communications have come some of our strong reasons for hope and confidence that the country will successfully meet its military challenges.

The Bell System is only one organization among many that are working for defense. We don't think we have all the answers. But we do think we ought to work for the answers the Government asks us to find in our particular field. And when we take on these assignments we share them as much as we possibly can with qualified subcontractors. Here in New York State, for example, some twelve hundred firms have been working with us in the past year as contractors and suppliers on military work.

All we want is to do our part, but to do that part fully. This is our duty and obligation, and it is shared by all telephone people. They understand that their individual acceptance of responsibility is vital to our total defense job. I think they would just want me to say without any fanfare, "We'll do our very best."

SURVIVABILITY OF COMMUNICATIONS

Armed Forces Communications and Electronics Association

WASHINGTON, D.C., JUNE 7, 1961

As I see it we are members of this Association for one purpose only. This is to make ourselves better able to contribute to the military strength and security of the United States. We civilians are members because we want to know military men and their problems, and in order that they may know our capabilities. We want to understand each other and also to stimulate each other. We want to bring out differences of opinion and judgment and get them resolved. But we don't want them resolved in your favor or my favor or anybody else's favor. We want them resolved in the country's favor, period.

To speak for the Bell System, I would like to indicate the nature and extent of our commitment as we see it today, and give a few examples of the effort we are making. While speaking on behalf of the organization I represent is as far as I can properly go, I am well aware that others in many fields have just as strong a sense of their defense obligations.

What we feel we must do can be stated with no ifs, ands, or buts. We must give the military what they need. I don't see any limiting qualifications here. I don't see how there could be any. This is the test and we cannot meet it with B or C grades. We have to get straight As.

The essence of private enterprise is clearly stated in the phrase itself—I mean enterprise, initiative, creativeness—everything a business will do to search for good answers on its own responsibility. It is this above all that the country needs from us in industry to help build our national strength.

It was in this spirit, for example, that we set out seven or eight years ago to build very extensive long distance communication routes avoiding designated critical target areas.

It is in the same spirit that we began construction last year of a new "hardened" cross-continent coaxial cable, entirely buried from end to end. This we are going ahead with at costs considerably higher than the costs of normal construction.

It is very much in the same spirit that we have pressed the development of new-type ocean cables and speeded up schedules for getting them into service. With *both* cable and satellite circuits in abundance, we shall get not only greater capacity but more firm assurance of reliability.

I give these examples to illustrate a point of view. We don't think these projects answer all the problems. Probably most people will agree that they are useful and important steps along the way. But like our friends in the Armed Forces, we in the Bell System are sharply aware that conditions are changing with great speed. We understand very well that the survivability of critical communications is all-important, and that attack on the communication system itself must not be permitted to succeed in its purpose. In short, we know how hot this griddle is. Our job is to improve and strengthen by every practical means the facilities we already have, and at the same time develop new ones.

Thus, to the diversity of the Direct Distance Dialing network we must add still more diversity. We must have more alternate routing of circuits by more effective means. We must work out means for more automatic restoral so that military networks will be self-healing to the highest degree possible.

The new cross-country cable system I mentioned will have all repeater and switching stations installed in heavily reinforced concrete underground vaults, and certain key stations will be manned around the clock. Before going ahead with this system, we tested the construction under blast conditions and found, for example, that the cable successfully withstood a pressure of well over two hundred pounds per square inch. The system can operate self-sufficiently on its own generated power and will have an ample water and reserve fuel supply.

In our work with satellites, we are intent on learning everything we can that will be useful for military communications, and we shall certainly expect to co-operate with the Armed Forces in all appropriate ways. Recently we testified before the House Committee on Science and Astronautics on the urgency of creating a satellite system to help meet military as well as other government and public demands.

A month or so ago we had a meeting of the presidents of all the Bell System companies. One of the subjects was our responsibilities for defense communications. Just for emphasis, I would like to tell you some of the main questions we pressed on each other. Here they are:

To begin with, are we making speed our watchword? And this means speed in all its aspects: Speed in ascertaining the military's needs. Speed, the utmost speed, in establishing the vital connection. Speed in developing new devices and systems. Speed in producing them and getting them in being.

Then to go on with our questions:

Are we further extending and increasing facilities that bypass military targets?

Are we providing sufficient hardening and fallout protection at appropriate locations? And are we developing improved designs for hardened plant?

What is the best balance of hardening, redundancy or diversity in the network, and mobility?

Are we generating realistic studies of survivable communications for military command and control, learning to pinpoint where the greatest needs lie, and striving to develop new modes of communicating?

Are we giving full and proper consideration to more extensive alternate routes, and ways to get them into action sooner in emergencies?

Are we doing all we ought to do in designing dedicated military networks that provide priority and automatic restoral, permit the encrypting of voice and data when desired, and afford the utmost measure of reliability and flexibility required for critical command?

And underlying and paralleling these and other efforts, are we at all times working closely with our military customers to know their needs and problems better?

I have repeated these questions here as partial evidence of the degree to which military concerns are our deep concern in the Bell System. We have no thought except to answer them well. That goes for the cost of service as well as its quality and reliability. Serving the Armed Forces as efficiently as possible is a clear obligation and we intend to meet it.

I would also like to say to our military friends that we welcome the pressures you put us under. This does not mean that in a different kind of world we would prefer the problems of defense to the arts of peace. The needs of defense are a gigantic burden on the whole country. Nevertheless the burden is inescapable and as long as that is so we want to tote our share as well as we can. In research and development work, the jobs you assign us sharpen our cutting edge. The same is true of skills in manufacture and operating competence. Everything you require of us helps our abilities in all our work. We want assignments from you, we intend to compete for them, and we welcome your demanding exactitude. But I don't expect you ever to be satisfied. If you ever are, that would really worry me.

The fundamental concern of all of us regarding military communications is survivability. If this country should be attacked, then without question critical communications must survive if the nation is to survive. It is clear therefore that every feasible technical step to insure survivability must be employed. But at the same time, in addition to technical and physical improvements, let us also remember human experience and human competence, well organized and often tested under conditions of emergency.

I am not so misguided as to attempt to compare the situation under a hydrogen bomb attack with past emergencies caused by earthquakes, hurricanes, floods, and other disasters. Nevertheless, the fact remains that many thousands of telephone people all over this country are trained and conditioned to deal with the unexpected, whatever it may be. They have a vast amount of knowledge and down-to-earth operating skill. They have an attitude, a natural disposition and instinct, to fix whatever may go wrong. They also have some other extremely important assets. For one thing, they have immediate authority to act—every test center, for instance, can act immediately. Second, they have detailed, specific programs as to what to do under differing circumstances. Third, a nationwide pool of materials, equipment, and other skilled people is available to help.

Without in the slightest degree minimizing the problems, I just hope that no one will underestimate what I will call the human resilience of the communications industry. For three generations or more, men and women in all the communications companies have co-operated effectively in protecting vital service against hazards of many kinds. This has left its mark on us as individuals and as an industry. It is a good mark and we are going to keep it so. In my judgment no single thing is more important to the survival of communications and the continuity of command.

Education and Management

FROM THE WORLD OF COLLEGE TO THE WORLD OF WORK

Westminster College
Fulton, Missouri

APRIL 5, 1962

THE general theme of this talk grows out of my deep concern for excellence in management, and my conviction that those who are to manage tomorrow's enterprise will need to do so superlatively well. I think the subject comes under the broad charter of these lectures because our national progress, our success in dealing with international problems, our ability to compete in world markets, and our success also in assisting in the development of better living standards in many other countries, all demand the best management of which we are capable.

To have a part in significant enterprise, to be one of its movers and managers, in industry or in government, is not to fill some niche each morning, and leave it each night as you found it. It is to help build and shape, to plan and to execute, to measure alternatives against the horizon and act on the course that judgment and resolution commend. It is to know that you and those who are working with you are accountable for the quality of change, and to develop every resource at your disposal in order to discharge such responsibility as well as you know how.

I do not hesitate to say that business should aspire to greatness, and search diligently for men who will make and keep it great. In numbers, the men who are needed to achieve this can not be counted in dozens, or in hundreds, but in many thousands. Ability and dedication are needed all through a business, not just in the topmost layer. And it is here, right here, that I come to our greatest concern in the business I am in. This is to develop and apply better, surer methods for drawing in and building up the people who can manage the Bell System more effectively in the future than we are doing it today.

We cannot be content to trust to luck here. I think we must admit that in the past, to a considerable extent, we have been flying by the seat of our pants. There must be better ways to travel.

I can see three avenues for improvement.

First, how can we better identify *today* who the young people are that can make tomorrow what it ought to be? How can we better predict what a man is likely to do and become?

Second, how can we improve our concepts and tactics of management, so that our ways of working will stimulate men more and hinder them less?

Third, how can we better judge the developing talents of different individuals so that all talent will be used to best advantage?

Since the war, we in the Bell System have hired as many as three thousand college men in a single year. And in doing this we have talked and talked with many thousands more. What has been the result?

First of all, we have hired a great many fine men. Second, we have also had some disappointing and disquieting experience. Third, we have been made very uneasy, to say the least, by a point of view that a great many young people have made only too clear.

I will call this point of view diplomaship, or addiction to the formula, "from sheepskin to job to success." Under this formula, the purpose of going to college is to get a degree, and the degree, I am sorry to say, is a passport to security.

The thousands of interviews we have had with young men, and our experience with a not inconsiderable number whom we have hired, have brought home to us that among many of them, this misconception is deeply lodged. I do not know the reason for this. I can only ask: Are the schools doing all they can to create a different view? Is the educational process itself organized to motivate, to inspire, to build and test men's full capacity and their will to make the most of themselves and give of their very best?

It hardly needs saying that the attitude of diplomaship is altogether different from the attitude needed to build vital, progressive industry and a greater nation. In searching out men who will be builders, I am sure there is no substitute for good judgment in the people who do the searching. But do we have anything else that can aid in the search?

Study of Actual Experience

In the Bell System, we have thought we should study the actual experience of college graduates in our business, in quantitative terms, and see whether this might help to point our noses in the right direction. And a generation ago, testing our intuition, we made a first effort to find out what relationship there might be, if any, between the performance of college graduates in the Bell System and their scholastic performance in college. The results showed that, proportionately, good scholars had progressed further in our management than poor ones.

In recent years we have made a similar study on a broader scale. We took the records of seventeen thousand college men in the business who could fairly be compared with each other, and examining their records sought the answer to the question: "To what extent does success in college predict success in the Bell System?"

As the criterion of success in the business, we used men's salaries. What was a man's salary compared to the salaries earned by others who had been working in the company for the same length of time? This criterion was used simply because a man's pay reflects the judgment of his bosses concerning his value to the company.

I realize these judgments are sometimes off the mark, both up and down. But considering the whole group of men whose records we have analyzed, I know of no measure that would better reflect their responsibilities in the business, relative to each other, than the salaries paid.

To measure college experience we considered, first, a man's academic achievements; second, his extracurricular achievement; third, the extent to which he earned his way.

Now for the results:

The figures show that the single most reliable predictive indicator of a college graduate's success in the Bell System is his rank in his graduating class. A far greater proportion of high-ranking than low-ranking students have qualified for the larger responsibilities. Forty-five per cent of the men in the top academic third were in our top salary third; while of those in the lowest third of their graduating classes, only 26 per cent made the top salary third.

Here is a parallel indicator: Only 21 per cent of the top-third students were in the bottom salary third, but 40 per cent of those in the lowest third at school were also in the lowest third in salary. That is a difference of almost two to one.

Since academic ranking might not mean the same thing from college to college, we checked out our figures against college quality. The colleges were grouped in three classes—above average, average, and below average. This grouping was based on years of association with the many colleges from which men come to us; on discussions with a number of college authorities; and on published studies.

We found that college quality does make a difference. For instance, 55 per cent of the men who ranked in the top third in the "above-average" group of colleges were in our top salary third, and 31 per cent in the lowest academic third made the top salary third. We also found, however, that top students from average or below-average colleges have done better than average or low-ranking students from above-average colleges. In short, while a relationship does exist between college quality and salary, rank in class is more significant. Our figures do *not* say to us that we should look for men only in the so-called "above-average" schools. On the contrary, the man and what he has done are much more important than where he did it.

Next, what about extracurricular achievement? Well, the data show some relationship between a high level of nonacademic achievement and salary later attained. Men who were campus leaders reached our top salary third in slightly greater proportion than those who were not. But it is only real campus achievement that seems to have any significance. Mere participation in extracurricular goings on does not.

Finally, if a man earns part or all of his college expenses, does that help us to gauge whether he will be successful in our business? The facts show that this by itself is not a significant yardstick. Please don't misunderstand me. Plenty of men who worked their way through school have worked their way up in the Bell System. But taking as a group all men who earned college expenses, they are in our different salary thirds in much the same proportion as men who did not.

Implications of the Study

Now I have given you the main facts. Do they mean that we should now proceed to offer jobs indiscriminately to anyone who happens to be in the top third or top half of his graduating class? Of course not. That would be absurd. There are top students who could no more be good business managers than I could read Chinese. Furthermore I expect most of these men are smart enough to know it.

What we have here are some rather strong hints about where to spend the most time looking for the men we do want, the men with intelligence *plus* those other attributes that give you the feel, the sense, the reasonable confidence that they will make things move and move well. And I will tell you what these statistical guide lines mean to us today: They mean that more and more, we are disposed to look *within* the top half of the college class for the individuals to whom we will offer career opportunities. We haven't yet gone all the way on this, but that is the general direction.

No one can dispute that many below-average students may become above-average managers. And admittedly there are men who make low grades in college but have plenty of brains. Nevertheless, we who employ college graduates must be concerned with the relative probability. Hiring the wrong man is costly in time, effort, and money, frustrating to all concerned, and dangerous for the future. There will always be some mistakes made in the hiring of people. The question is how can we make as few mistakes as possible? And how can we disregard the evidence that confronts us?

When you hire a man of high intelligence but low grades, in effect you have to bet that a drive he hasn't yet shown *will* show after he goes to work. If, on the other hand, you are considering a high-scholarship man, your bet is that a drive already demonstrated will be sustained.

Of course, there are other equally important factors, integrity, creativity, personality characteristics. But these you must judge in both cases anyway.

Suppose you were weighing the choice. Which way would you lean if you were hiring thousands of college men? Sometimes our college employment people pick lower-scholarship men, *but they need to feel strongly that other factors justify this,* for they know they are betting against the odds.

And here I will make a personal guess with no statistics at all to back me up. My guess is that there are many more representatives of the diplomaship formula down in the lower ranks of college classes than there are on the top side. So I put it to you: As we look for career managers, why should we spend a large part of our effort searching among men who have made a career of just getting by? The proper goal of a business can't be just to get by. No enterprise with that object in life will be able to do what the times demand. But if we should content ourselves with get-by people, that is the way they would shape the business.

Now there is another side to all this, and that is how a business influences men after it employs them. So we come to these questions: How can we better judge the developing talents of different men so that all talents will be used to best advantage? How smart are we in bringing out a man's best?

I wish we could say that every boss had the savvy needed to help and inspire everybody who worked for him, and the insight to judge his men well. But this is not the way things are. Too many bosses cling to established methods of working just because these methods have been successful in the past. Not enough of them realize that helping tomorrow's managers grow is one of their prime responsibilities. Too few have the ability to discern potential talent and then test and release it.

A Long-Range Analysis

Naturally you keep trying every way you can to get these things done better. But tonight I want to tell you briefly about just one of the efforts we are making, for this is a bit unusual.

About six years ago we started a long-range study of the experience and performance of a group of 425 young managers in six of the Bell telephone companies. The idea was to learn everything we can about each one of them—his personal assets and liabilities, changes in his point of view, the step-by-step influence of his experience on his character and capabilities. To get this knowledge, experienced management men and a group of psychologists work closely together.

The men who entered the study were first examined and tested every which way, physically and mentally, during a period of several days. Then they were carefully rated.

Each year thereafter, each man has been interviewed. These interviews review in detail the man's experience and progress, his successes and failures, his hopes and his goals. Every several years it is planned to repeat the full assessment.

All the information obtained is kept in confidence at an independent research institute, and each man knows that nothing pertaining to him as an individual will be reported. Also, we realize that when you study a group of men, this in itself tends to have some influence on them. We do all we can to minimize this.

Now, what are we getting out of this undertaking? The short answer is that we get a much more thorough, complete knowledge of a group of men in our business than we ever had before. The purpose of course is to use this knowledge to do a better job not only in hiring but also in developing tomorrow's managers.

What we have learned so far strongly supports our conclusion that scholarship *is* a good indicator of business success. We have also learned that many of the men thought our initial training procedures were dull and boring. So in several of the Bell companies, we have been working toward a quite different way of starting college graduates off.

The usual practice has been to assign a man temporarily to first one department, then another, so that he could get a general picture of the business. Then, after quite a few months of this, he is given a real job to do. The experimental program is quite different. The new man gets one week of initial training. Then he is assigned to a manager who has extensive responsibilities, and the latter *immediately* gives him a real job to perform. This is not "made work," but something that needs to be done and demands right away the level of intellectual effort and application that the recent graduate has been trained for. Of course the manager supervises and gives direction; but the responsibility is the man's, and he knows that what he is called on to do is a regular, necessary part of our business operation. This is still training, but with a difference. Naturally the man who gets an assignment under these conditions has an immense amount to learn; but the basic concept is that when he has to get a real job accomplished, this will greatly increase his motivation to learn, for he *must* learn many things in order to carry out the mission.

This kind of initial training has spread quite a bit in our business in the last few years. You might well ask, "Why shouldn't it? It only seems like common sense." I feel that way about it too. It certainly checks with my own early experience, when I was fortunate enough to have bosses who didn't waste any time in giving me real jobs to do. But the point here is to work things around so that good and exciting early experience will be less a matter of chance, less hit-or-miss.

Assessment for Promotion

A third result of our study of the 425 men was not foreseen when we started it. You will remember I said that the men went through a thorough assessment by experienced management men and psychologists. This includes the assignment of real-life management problems of the kind we have to deal with in our business every day. The men work on these problems under observation and each man's performance is carefully rated.

Some plant department managers in one of the Bell companies heard about this and asked if the same procedure couldn't be tried with employees who were being considered for promotion to the first level of management. To make a long story short, this was done and the results were eye opening. It was found that a high proportion of the men under consideration simply did not qualify for supervisory jobs.

Today these assessment procedures are being used at seventeen locations throughout the country to help management do a more selective, more careful job in promoting employees from the ranks. By such means the local managers of the business are much better able to reach right decisions and avoid costly mistakes in evaluating people.

All of this, as I indicated, comes out of our study of the 425 men. And a point worth stressing is this: To improve your attack on hard problems, sometimes it helps greatly to take very special steps. This study, for example, is a piece of long-range research. Yet the knowledge it is yielding has already pushed many managers in our business into new, more promising action.

When we know just how and why men succeed or fail, then we can systematically compare this knowledge with what we knew about them when they were first hired. Using these findings, we then hope to be able to make better judgments in choosing men for high-level jobs as well as for their earlier management jobs. And to refer again to the initial hiring, we shall be better able to choose between good students who would not do well in our business and those who are more likely to succeed.

All through this talk I have been discussing two aspects of a single basic question: How do we continuously keep building the best management we can? One aspect is the preparation for the future that men obtain in their college experience. The second aspect is our own responsibility to help men develop their powers after they have joined the business. Everyone of course cannot be in the top tenth, quarter, or half of any organization, and it is not to be thought that any individual is intrinsically more important than another. The need is for everyone's best according to his abilities. But these alone should mark the boundaries of a man's progress, and his course should be as little affected as possible by luck and by other people's superficial judgments.

To conclude now, I strongly believe, as I said at the start, that genuine excellence in management is vital to the nation's welfare and to our competence and leadership in world affairs. In our time too many people have come to see their futures in terms of circumstances outside themselves, in terms of an institution that will do something for them. This value is upside down. The future must be seen in terms of what a man can do to contribute something, to make something better, to make it go where he believes with all his being that it ought to go. Opportunity is not so much in the situation, as in the enthusiasm, the intelligence, the judgment and courage that men bring *to* the situation. Where do interest, vitality, the sense of challenge, and ethical awareness come from? Are these things that work gives to a man? No, they are not. These are things that men bring to work. And when education, business, and government all reinforce each other's efforts to help men grow as bringers, then and only then, I believe, we shall have excellence.

THREE QUESTIONS FOR THE BUSINESS SCHOOLS

Whittemore School of Business and Economics University of New Hampshire

MARCH 28, 1963

I WOULD hope that the school of business—this school, or any other—would see its role as being essentially to turn out graduates who have not merely a certain competence, or a certain training that will be useful in the vocations they select, but who have, more importantly, the drive and enthusiasm to make things move; the will to grow up and step up to responsibilities of large importance. To my mind it is these character qualities in individual people that we must have to make a free economy dynamic, and keep a dynamic economy free.

I don't see how a businessman can contribute to this end if he is not dedicated to manage his business toward accomplishment tomorrow that cannot be achieved today. I don't see how a student can look forward to contributing if he doesn't feel a certain excitement in his blood. I don't see how a school can help much if it doesn't have a mission to get young people stirred up about what a free economy can be, can do, can bring to pass—if it doesn't get them asking, "How much a part of this can I be? How far in responsibility can I go? And how do I equip myself?"

Further, it seems to me that to bring about this kind of attitude, business educators and business leaders have to share a real brotherhood of interest.

Today we are dedicating a school of business and economics where before there had been a department of the University. This very fact, I choose to believe, signifies New Hampshire's understanding that the mission I speak of is important, and needs to be carried out.

The fact that formal business education is not indispensable does not limit its potential. It might even be said to increase it. For the doors to the future are wide open. There are fewer traditions but more creative possibilities. The challenge and the need to innovate press upon the business school as they press on business itself. And just as business organizations must demonstrate accomplishments that are persuasive of their worth and mettle, so too, I think, the schools of business must also persuade by demonstration in order to make their way.

Developing a Sound Basic Attitude

The first need I see is to give young people who aspire to management careers a realistic view of the opportunities ahead of them, and how they need to grow and develop in preparation for management responsibility. For even the most talented individual, if his expectations are fanciful and unrealistic, may find himself in confusion when he lands in business. He may go down wrong avenues and his full capabilities may never emerge.

A great many young people need to sense more accurately, before they go to work, what is required to become a good manager. In the business I am in we talk with thousands who have their careers on their minds, and it seems to us that a large proportion of them have wrong notions. They have fixed ideas about being financial men, or marketing specialists, or statisticians, or about playing some other particular role. But if a person wants to develop himself as a manager, then *management competence*—just that—should be his aim. Fixed ideas that may have crystallized out of the study of specialized subjects will only interfere.

Specialized knowledge is useful and important, and often a person may make his best long-run contribution to a business in some specialized role. But not by letting the specialty, whatever it is, determine his outlook prematurely. Rather, he needs to learn from experience how to use his knowledge in the context of the management task.

So I think the realistic young person is the one who says to himself, "I want to learn to manage, and I can only learn this from actual experience. This is what I need. This is what I want. This is what I am determined to do—to learn to manage, by managing."

In my judgment this is the first basic attitude that an ambitious and capable individual should have when he enters a business—any business.

Management competence is many things. Part of it is mastering the clear technical requirements of knowledge and skill (including I suspect in the future more skill in mathematics and systematic analysis than was required in the past). But the hardest part to acquire is more subtle: I mean the intuitive grasp of how things relate to each other, how these relationships are likely to change, the sense of timing, a feeling for people, firmness when needed, patience when needed, courage when needed. And there is another critical requirement, I want to add. This is to be able to earn the respect and co-operation of the people you work with. No matter how smart a man is, to a great extent his success depends on other people. Sometimes men of great personal talent fail simply because they will not understand this, and cannot win the co-operation of others.

The basic attitudes and expectations that influence the development of management competence are set partly in school. And the business schools, it seems to me, could be particularly effective in helping the student get rid of false expectations. They could help him understand better what the essential requirements of managing are, and how he can grow so as to master them.

The Sense of Responsibility

The second question I submit as a matter of critical concern to business and business schools alike is the sense of public responsibility.

No one could believe more wholeheartedly in private enterprise than I do. But no enterprise is so private that it can do without public spirit. Financial incentives and rewards are essential to bring out good performance. Any business must meet the criterion of profitability if it is to contribute something to the economy and not be a drag on it. However, profitability is not the only criterion, and the purpose of business is not simply to provide the opportunity for making a fast buck.

Let us ask ourselves: Why does any business exist? From one point of view, to succeed financially, to earn a good healthy profit, to grow, to prosper. Naturally. If it can't do these things it can't go very far and it may go down the drain.

From the same kind of viewpoint, an individual gets a job to make a living, to get ahead, to be self-supporting and look after his family. All these goals spur personal achievement.

But there is another viewpoint as well. This is the social view, and it says that the basic reason for any job, and for any business, is to get work done, to produce the goods and services the community needs, to create things that have public value. This view is fundamental. It is deeper than the profit view. It is why we know in the telephone business, for example, that we have only one license to exist, which is to give good service.

Some may say that the pursuit of private gain is all that is needed to produce the public value, that the sense of public responsibility has nothing to do with it. I do not agree with this. I think we need more feeling of responsibility and less of "What's in it for me and how can I get it quickly?"

The fast-buck philosophy not only stands in the way of a good job, it robs the individual of the sense of accomplishment that he needs in his personal life. I don't mean a person has to be a "do-gooder" in the sense in which that phrase is often used. But he ought to approach business life with the idea that he has obligations to fulfill, and that good management, sound business practice, and balanced judgment are ideals well worth his best striving.

I would urge on the business schools, therefore, that they do all they can to get the sense of public responsibility operating in people before they go to work.

Ethical Conduct

The third question on my mind is closely related to the other two. This is the matter of business ethics.

We have heard a good deal about business ethics in the last few years. And some people have had the idea that if every business only had some kind of ethical rulebook to go by, that would improve corporate morals.

I have no objection to ethical maxims, but I don't think they contribute much to ethical conduct. To me, the important thing is what is inside individual people. Ethical conduct is partly wanting very strongly to do the right thing. It is partly a drive to get knowledge and experience so that errors and failure can be prevented. It is partly dogged persistence in staying with a problem until a right answer can be worked out. All of which means that being ethical is difficult. You have to work at it constantly and you can't stop for a breather. But I don't know anyone who works at it the way I have described who wouldn't say, "It's worth it."

Now, I think you can do something about this in a business school. It will probably be the more difficult in the case of students who didn't get their ethical sights set reasonably high when they were young. Yet if their sights are low, that in itself would seem to make the need for your effort more urgent.

Just what form the effort might take I leave to you. But so far as I know, the drive toward ethical conduct comes basically out of religion, or if you want me to put it more broadly, out of mankind's concern with the ultimate meaning of life. This is the fundamental source. I do not say that you should teach religion or philosophy in a business school. I do suggest however that to concern yourselves effectively with the ethical development of students, to have some success in raising the level of ethical aspiration, then one way or another it is necessary to bring them to the source, the fountainhead.

In business this is hard to do. We must strive for ethical conduct by precept and example, and by holding people to account. But the shaping of basic beliefs belongs to the home, the church, the school. And in this field, it seems to me, you in the schools have great opportunity and responsibility to be leaders who will exert influence over the whole business community.

Now I have given you a large order. First is the development of more realistic concepts by young people of how they can best realize their potential as business managers. Second is the development of a greater sense of public responsibility. And third, the instilling of ethical values.

All these needs have to do with attitudes and character formation, rather than with vocational skills and knowledge of the business process. I do not slight the latter. They are very important. But it is how well we form character, and establish attitudes that open the way to full personal growth, that will be decisive for the future of American business and American society. Are we producing enough realistic, responsible people who can carry heavy burdens in all walks of life? I seriously doubt it. I believe this must be a matter of concern to every person and organization that has the chance to tackle some part of the problem. And it is only if the business schools will take on the attitude and character questions, and demonstrate results, that I think they will be truly persuasive, in the sense in which I use that word.

PERSONNEL MANAGEMENT

Industrial College of the Armed Forces

JANUARY 7, 1964

ESSENTIALLY, the handling of people is every boss's job. And the basic principle, it seems to me, is always to think of the man—or the woman—in relation to the work and vice versa. We mustn't ever let the two get separated. Never think of a man except in relation to his work and its value to the enterprise. Never think of the work without respecting the man who does it as a unique human being.

This is the heart of personnel management. We are never perfect at it. In the short run, sometimes the work may suffer a bit when a man is sick or upset or doesn't know what to do; but if he's a good man we invest something in him. Sometimes, on the other hand, the work becomes so urgent that the man may suffer—the strain is wearing, or some other important aspect of life has to be temporarily neglected, or some personal need must be put off longer than it really should be. But in the long run the work must be done well, *and* the man must fare well as a human being. These two must be in balance. Neither part can be served for long at the expense of the other. In a sound business, both must be served well.

Wages, benefits, health and safety, selection, development, placement—these are all concerned with getting people into position to do their work and sustaining them there. They are all important and necessary, but they will not by themselves get us where we want to go. For that, I will stress two other things that deal with the work itself.

The first is standards of performance. People must be clear as to what is expected of them and how they are to be judged.

The most discouraging kind of work is where the aims are fuzzy or the judgment on the job is inexact. A man needs to know, beforehand, what he is supposed to do, and after the fact he needs to know how well he is judged to have done it. Really, nothing else in personnel management counts more than this.

The second main aspect of personnel management that deals with the work is leadership and direction. An awful lot is wrapped up in those two words. Once a business knows where it is going and what people must do to get there, the leadership of management at all levels is what takes it there.

This is not a talk on leadership specifically, but I will say this much about it:

Leadership is stirring people so that they are moved from inside themselves. It is stating goals that excite them and lift their sights. It is setting the personal example, putting enthusiasm into the operation, communicating both ways (listening as well as talking). It is rewarding merit and penalizing demerit, honestly and fairly. It is the right combination of these so that people will do the work that makes a business successful *because they want to.*

Five Dimensions

So the main dimensions of the personnel management job as I see them are:

First, the basic principle that personnel management is every boss's job.

Second, that you always look at a man and his work together, and never separate the two.

Third, the various conditions and factors involved in getting people into position to do their work and sustaining them there.

Fourth, the necessity for clear standards of performance.

Fifth, the function of leadership.

But all these things together merely help us to see what the job is. And seeing is the easy part. The tough question is: how do you get an organization to do well at these things from the time you hire a man to the time he leaves you? Particularly, how do you get a big organization with several levels of management to do well at it?

I will start with this thought: A going business, such as the one I am in, has its way of doing things, its policies, its goals—some long established. And in this tradition some things are timeless—in the Bell System, for example, what we call the spirit of service; the standards of character and morals in our dealings within the business and outside; our commitment to research and innovation, to efficiency and constant improvement of service.

Now all these things grow out of how people think and work. It is the dealings of people with each other that make the tradition. The point I would stress here is simply that so much of this starts right at the top of the organization. If there is not a strong interest and influence at the top, and if the top thinking is not right, it is very hard for the rest of the operation to be right. For instance, if decisions made at the top of the organization on the selection and development of people are not good, it will be mighty tough to get good decisions anywhere. Momentum may carry the business over an occasional mistake, but in the long run, if the top direction is not of a high order, nothing else will be of a high order either. Furthermore, this kind of work cannot be delegated the way many other assignments are delegated—the top people personally *have* to make the decisions that will largely shape all personnel management throughout the company.

Now I have talked about tradition and about the prime responsibility that rests on top management. But of course I do not mean that all you have to do is fall in line with tradition, and neither do I mean that the top people can do the whole personnel job by themselves. The tradition is always being modified—in fact it is the quality of innovation that keeps the timeless things lively. Also, the line management, at the top and at all levels, needs good staff help. I would say it needs staff help of particularly high quality, because it is harder really to know about people than to know about any other aspect of a business. It is not infrequently hard to know about some of the people you are directly associated with—and much harder to know about large numbers whom you never get to see.

A Key Role for Personnel People

In our business, the personnel staff organization has a broad range of responsibilities in administering wage practices, pensions and benefits, health programs, and so on. These are all important, but in my mind the personnel people have another key role that could be, and I think ought to be, increasingly influential in the years ahead. It seems to me it ought to be always their job to keep looking at all these aspects of personnel management I have spoken of and to come up with sound, thoughtful, practical ideas for doing them better. They should be researchers and educators. They should be scanning the horizon, looking ahead, and doing the kind of thinking that a busy operating man does not have time for. The operating manager shouldn't have to keep needling them to look at this or that problem, to map out a good solution, to get the necessary knowledge that will lead to useful action; they should be doing these things and be able to prove why they ought to be done. They should be so completely competent at this that they will have no trouble commanding respect. The sum of all their effort ought to make theirs the wisest and most sought-after counsel on personnel matters. When they recommend some action, they ought to know, better than anyone else, just what it may be expected to accomplish; and then if the action is taken they ought to be able to tell us just what in fact it did accomplish. Now I haven't said anything that isn't just as applicable to any other staff function.

To recapitulate again, very briefly:

For a good job of personnel management, the first need is for a chief executive and a top management group that *want* a good job and have the ability to get that kind of job started by reason of their own intuitive understanding and good performance in decisions affecting people.

The second need is for staff help that is demonstrably first-class—strong, imaginative, practical, persuasive people who are devoted to improving performance, who know how to get the necessary knowledge, and who are able to put their recommendations across.

In a very real sense, I think of good personnel management as a war against bureaucracy, and one of the tests I constantly make in my own mind about the effectiveness of the personnel job is whether it is being done in a way that makes us more bureaucratic or less so. I know an organization can't run without rules, and all that, but we simply have to keep fighting this tendency on the part of many management people to depend on precedent, to be rigid in their thinking.

And this is not just a matter of the petty red-tape items that slow down work and make it more expensive and less effective. It is much more than that—it is the negative habit of mind that is deadly. I spoke earlier of tradition, and I set great store by tradition. But the tradition has to be dynamic, not static, it has to be continuously modified and revised. In fact, it seems to me reasonable to think of all staff work as a continuous effort to revise tradition, to keep pumping new life into it; and perhaps this is especially true in personnel management, because here we are dealing with the human and personal factors that really create the tradition.

Another consequence of bureaucracy is that almost by definition it tends to prevent communication, the free give-and-take of ideas. Sure, there can be lots of pieces of paper with writing on them, but they and the talking all flow in one direction. Because the easy way, the bureaucratic way, is just to pass out the work—and a few yards of advice along with it. The hard way, apparently, is to listen and discuss with the people who are doing the work. But without listening and discussion of the issues in the work and in the business, pretty soon we lose the cement of understanding that is absolutely necessary. Human beings simply do not function well if all of the communication is in the "telling." How to check this tendency and get real communication in a big organization that is busy as a beehive with a lot of things to do is one of the toughest problems of personnel management I know about. But it has to be done and done well, and while the cost in time and dollars may be high, so far as I am concerned this is one of the essential costs of doing business.

Two Talks at Life Insurance Gatherings

EQUITABLE LIFE ASSURANCE SOCIETY

Life Insurance Symposium

NEW YORK, JULY 28, 1959

THERE is one aspect of life insurance that I wish could be given a more lively understanding among people who hold individual life policies. Every policyholder has a personal stake in business and in the success of our whole enterprise system. A good big part of every premium he pays gets invested in this or that company in this or that industry. And later on, the benefits that he or his beneficiaries receive are paid out of the fruits of enterprise. Yet I doubt that the average person who carries life insurance has a very strong or acute sense of just what it is that makes his policy possible and enables him to put his faith in it.

Many millions of Americans hold life policies. The more we can bring home to them that the strength of their policies and the strength of private enterprise are two sides of the same thing, the better they will understand the need for a political climate that fosters and encourages enterprise, and the wiser will be their judgments—and their votes.

We in the Bell System have had a long-standing interest in encouraging the life insurance idea. I really don't see how our business, or most any other business for that matter, could function as it does if the people who carry on the business didn't have access to life insurance.

The fact is, in our society most people don't have the resources that will enable them to take on responsibilities without worrying about the risks of the future. A couple of hundred years ago, when most people lived on the land, the land was their insurance. Today industry is really the insurance and the practical access to a piece of it is through the insurance policy. This I think is indispensable to providing a reasonable sense of protection against future hazards, so that a person can wholeheartedly bend his mind and energy to the work at hand.

You often hear it said that many people today are too much concerned with security. I agree that to achieve a cozy security is not much of an ambition, and I think those people are dead right who say that if that is all we are after, then we are sunk.

However, just because security is sometimes overemphasized doesn't mean that men and women can get along without a reasonable amount of it. This is a basic human need. The great thing about life insurance is that it gives us a practical way to put security in its place, so to speak. We can take care of some of these problems that would otherwise be always nagging at us, and then with reasonable peace of mind we can get on with our jobs.

Moreover, going down the life insurance road means that a man is working to build his own security and is not just looking to somebody else to build it for him. Life insurance invites personal initiative as the means to build security, and this it seems to me is exactly the right way to go about it. At the same time, the savings that are created get invested in other enterprise, and we have this circle in which each step keeps stimulating the next step. In effect, what we have is a process that transforms the drive for security into a drive for growth, for expansion, for progress. What benefits the individual in one way benefits industry and society in another, and this is surely what we all want.

If I have studied my lessons correctly, insurance got started many years ago as a means for enabling people to take risks they would otherwise have shied away from. This was not life insurance, it was shipping cargoes at sea. However, the basic principle at work in life insurance is much the same. With life insurance we can take on responsibilities that might otherwise seem forbidden to us. We can act instead of hesitating to act. We can move instead of standing still. We can concentrate on our goals instead of consulting our fears. The very principle of life insurance is to do, to work, to venture, to set out on a journey. What this means to industry, which is wholly dependent on how intensely the people in it want to journey forth, is beyond all calculation.

I think life insurance will be more and more needed in years to come. This moves me to say strongly that I hope everyone in the industry will do as much as he can to fight inflation. As we all know, inflation robs every man who uses his savings to insure his life and the welfare of his family. I urge therefore that all life insurance people do their utmost to talk down and argue down and vote down practices and policies that feed inflation.

The leaders of the industry, as I know from acquaintance with many of them, are the first to understand the great danger that must be prevented. I hope they will spread this understanding to the limit. I hope they will resist this idea that the country should deliberately accept a little inflation as inevitable, and even as a good thing. Allen Sproul recently commented that to give such a policy public sanction would be to admit that our money economy has broken down. It seems to me that the life insurance companies, which are the very symbol of integrity in money matters, must be among the leaders in working to prevent this.

METROPOLITAN LIFE INSURANCE COMPANY

Managers' Convention

NEW YORK, MARCH 13, 1963

SINCE your subject this morning has been communication in the broad sense—I mean the flow of knowledge and ideas back and forth between people in the organization—Mr. Fitzhugh suggested I bring along a few thoughts about that.

I think the first question is—*why* do we in business want to communicate? What do we want communication to *do*?

The answer as I conceive it is very simple. We need communication to promote the future welfare and usefulness of the business. We want knowledge and ideas to flow so that the people in the organization can contribute more effectively toward its success.

You may say this is obvious. But the point is, we have to have some criterion, some standard, to measure our efforts against. We have to test the value of our communicating. We can raise a great wind of communication and blow a lot of leaves around. But if the whole effort isn't rightly suited to promote the future welfare and usefulness of the business, we won't have much to show for all our trying.

Now, if this settles the question of why we communicate, we can proceed to the questions of what and how.

In my judgment, the first thing a business needs to communicate to all the people in it is a sense of its purposes and goals. I mean a lively awareness of what the business is driving at, and a sense of excitement and pride in helping to bring it about.

We want people to feel this personally, so that they will be determined, in fact dedicated, to accomplish the goals of the business. We want to help them grow in enthusiasm as well as ability. We can be confident too, I think, that the people who grow in this way will best serve their own satisfaction.

If I say a word here about Bell System experience, it isn't because I think we are ahead of other businesses in accomplishing such results. We are keenly aware of our problems. Yet I am sure that whatever success we have had, insufficient as it may be, has had its roots in the process of setting demanding, challenging goals.

These are old-fashioned adjectives but they are necessary. The goals *must* be demanding, they *must* be challenging. Easy goals do not stimulate people. Little goals do not produce big striving.

How a Big Goal Spurs Effort

Three quarters of a century ago or longer, the people who were setting the Bell System in motion were also setting an astounding goal. They were looking ahead to universal telephone service, so that anyone could talk to anyone else. In 1885, for example, the charter of the A. T. & T. Company said the company would be in business to connect every place in the country with other cities and towns all over the nation, "and by cable and other appropriate means, with the rest of the known world."

When these words were written the company just did not have the ability to make them come true. But the business had established a long course of future striving. It had a great goal to communicate. The effect of this in spurring people on has been beyond calculation.

One thing the big goal dramatized was the need for research and technical development. This was really the source of the first sustained effort by a business to get new scientific knowledge and apply it to business problems. For many years now, this effort has been a way of life with us, and I hope it always will be.

Today the goal of universal service has been largely realized within the United States. Yet worldwide service between continents and across oceans is still in a relatively early stage of development. Manifestly, it isn't our goal or ambition in the Bell System to provide service in other countries. And overseas service is a partnership matter, involving the communication companies and agencies of the various countries. However, we think it *is* a very lively goal for us to be leaders in creating worldwide communications that will meet future needs.

Another of today's goals in the Bell System is to bring about a new order of dependability in the service we provide. This is vitally important for defense reasons but there are other reasons too. The transmission of data requires electrical circuits of even better quality than are needed to carry the voice. Also, Direct Distance Dialing means that any trouble a customer runs into affects him directly and immediately, whereas in the past the operator could often overcome difficulties without the customer being much aware of it. With direct dialing we can give much faster service. But at the same time, we have to protect the customer, we have to perfect the service to the nth degree.

Another goal we have set for ourselves is to give people plenty of choice in buying their communication service. As you know, we don't have competition in our business in the sense of different telephone companies competing within the same area. But we certainly do want people to feel they can choose what they want from us, in the same way that they can choose between competitive products in a supermarket.

For instance, we can aim at giving particular people the particular telephones that please them most.

We can aim at providing most any kind of home or office communication system that any customer might want.

We can offer businessmen long distance calls paid for one at a time, or as many as they want to make, paid for by the month.

We can provide narrow communication channels or wide ones, for sending information in any amount and in every conceivable form.

And coming soon, with new electronic switching equipment we shall be able to provide new services, new features, new options of many kinds.

This goal of offering many choices is real, is important, and compels our best effort. All through our organization, we have something new to communicate, just as you have in Metropolitan when you develop new insurance programs, new values for your customers, and new methods for selling them.

I'd like to speak also of one other goal. This is to get a feeling for quality, an instinct for excellent performance, into people's bones. To me there is nothing more important. I think there is no aspect of our business where the goal of quality can be given second place.

Take a thing like the Telstar® satellite. It demands the highest quality of scientific, engineering, and manufacturing effort. The same is true of ocean cable amplifiers that are designed and built to operate without attention for twenty years or more at the bottom of the sea.

But the need for excellence is broader than this. It is everywhere. It is in the way a telephone installer does his job in your home. It is in the rating given our securities. It is in the maintenance of central office apparatus. It is in the appearance of our cars and trucks, and the character and dignity of our signs and advertisements. It is in how we splice wires, handle calls, and organize tomorrow's work and next year's financing. In sum, it is in how all of us do our jobs and how we conduct ourselves in every move we make.

Quality *makes* work worth doing. And the feeling for quality, once a man gets it in his bones, he will prize as one of his greatest assets. This gives dignity to the individual, character to the business, lasting substance to investment, and satisfaction to customers, with attendant public respect.

Processes of Communication

I'll turn now to the "how" of communication, the day-to-day processes involved.

Publication is very important, but publication is not, in itself, communication. Communication is what gets out of one mind and into another. This depends mainly on how bosses talk and listen and deal with the people who work for them, and on how they, in turn, talk and listen and deal with their bosses.

In these relationships, what sort of principles favor good communication?

Well, to begin with, if the purpose of communication is to improve the future welfare and usefulness of the business, then the communication between the boss and his people must have this purpose and no other. It is up to the boss to make clear that what he and all his employees must always be working for is the ability to do tomorrow what they have not yet learned to do today.

What I've already said about goals is also pertinent here. For it is self-evident that having a goal means you want to achieve capabilities that are beyond present reach.

I think this principle of improvement needs to be embedded in the communications between every boss and his people.

It requires the boss to think out what he wants, and why.

It makes him an educator, and he cannot be one without striving to educate himself.

It encourages recognition of good work, for the boss who really uses the principle of improvement will also be wise enough to let people know about their successes.

The same principle also requires continuous watching to put local goals and efforts into perspective with long-range company objectives. This is not a matter of loading all the big purposes of the business on local shoulders, but of showing how local performance contributes toward achieving them.

Then there is another thing that I think is tremendously important.

When a boss makes clear to his people that the purpose of all the communicating is to accomplish a better job, he sets a fine trap for himself. For then he has to listen to *their* ideas. He has to let them communicate to him.

No one disputes the proposition that what a business needs is two-way communication, communication back and forth and up and down. The problem is how to get it. And if we do not get it between the boss and the people who work for him, we will not get it at all. In fact, where else could we look for it?

The hopeful thing here is that the boss is constantly plagued by the need to make decisions. And in coming to decisions, any reasonably intelligent boss knows he can get more help from the people who work for him than he can from anyone else. In this fact lies one of the main hopes for effective two-way communication.

Such communication not only requires confidence and trust, it also helps to build them. Only the boss can know his employees' information needs. And listening may sometimes be more useful than anything he could say. It isn't necessary to run around informing all the time. Many communication needs are well satisfied simply by an atmosphere that tells people they may ask, comment, or suggest.

Now, I have stayed with a few fundamentals because I think we have to have principles working for us when we tackle the problems and snarls of communications in actual practice.

In big organizations especially, with several levels of management, ideas get altered and emphases changed as communications filter through many minds. People find, or think they find, conflicts between the expressed aims of the business and what they are asked to do. They hear the top bosses declaiming one thing and their immediate boss pressing for another. Beliefs can be shaken and management sincerity questioned. And, unfortunately, many bosses keep the avenues for upward communication closed.

Things to Be Done

We shall never get problems like these solved in one fell swoop. But there are things we can do.

We can take soundings from time to time to learn better what the people in the organization really do think; what their attitudes are; whether the ideas we are trying to communicate are being received; and in what ways conflicting pressures are producing uncertainties or confusion.

This must be done carefully. However, reliable information can be obtained and sound appraisals can be made.

Going on from there, we can be critical of our own faults in disseminating ideas.

We can take more pains to make ourselves more clear.

We can recognize that communication takes time as well as brains, and schedule work accordingly.

We can search hard for forms of organization that will foster better communication.

We can pin-point the places and groups where messages come through loud and clear. Why is there understanding in one part of the outfit and confusion in another? Where does the responsibility lie? How can we multiply our successes?

Where pressures *are* in conflict, we can, we must make changes.

Above all, we must bring up bosses who mean what they say and have the ability to prove it. There is no such thing as good tongue-in-cheek management, or a good keep-it-to-himself boss. In every business, people work best when the boss shares his thoughts and problems but not his responsibilities with them, and when they are convinced that what he says, he wholeheartedly means. If there are many keys to good communication, nevertheless this, I am sure, is the master key.

In conclusion, I have a few words about a particular opportunity for communication that you face as insurance people.

I think you have a duty to give millions of Americans a better understanding of what the success and profitability of private enterprise means to them personally.

There isn't one of your policyholders who doesn't have a personal stake in this. A sizable part of every premium paid is invested in industry. And later on, beneficiaries are paid out of the fruits of enterprise.

Yet how many are keenly aware that the security they are paying for depends on the profitability of the business? How many understand that this is the fuel for "The Light That Never Fails"?

It seems to me it is the obligation of insurance people, not only to sell insurance policies for all the good reasons you can give your clients for protecting themselves, but also to get across the truth about what makes the protection safe and sound. I think you need to make clear to people that as the volume of insurance grows, the overall volume of business profit must increase to support it.

Policyholders must understand that when they buy insurance, they are laying on the line their hope that profits *are* good and will stay good in relation to the increasing total of business investment. If they do not understand this, then it seems to me they have no realization of what they are doing when they place their trust in you.

Your watchword in this business has always been to provide safety and dependable protection. Isn't it your obligation, as you sell this protection, also to sell the basic ideas that must prevail to make your proposition everything you represent it to be?

I sincerely believe that if you would put this high on your own list of goals, more might be accomplished for the whole country than anyone here now imagines.

Commencement Addresses

LEHIGH UNIVERSITY

JUNE 9, 1958

IN the case of most of you here this morning, your working lives will extend right up to the year 2000. Quite a few of you will probably be working even longer. In any event, you are citizens not only of this century, but also of the next.

And I ask you: Is there one of you who does not feel in his bones that he will be witness to events of great moment and consequence? Is there anyone who doubts that this second half of the twentieth century will be a decisive period in the history of the world? Is there anyone who does not expect that his personal crossing into the twenty-first century will take him over seas of change?

It seems to me that in any direction we care to look, the future is asking for the best we have to give. Here are a few glances more or less at random:

1. We and the rest of the free nations are engaged in a struggle to maintain our freedom. Yet we are divided among ourselves; we have conflicting goals and aspirations, whereas the Communist world is relatively united. We need to achieve by voluntary means a unity which Communism brings about by force. For us in the United States, who now have a responsibility for leadership that is new to us, this is perhaps the greatest test we have ever faced.

2. In this country we are using up our natural resources. We shall have increasing need for raw materials from other countries. The fostering of international trade is essential to our economic progress. Yet we have tremendous difficulty in coming to reasonable agreement on economic policy.

3. We have a civil rights problem which calls for the utmost in wisdom and patience. How we conduct ourselves will deeply affect not alone our domestic welfare, but our prestige and influence throughout the world.

4. Our population has been growing fast. Up to now this has spurred our economy, and I hope and expect that it will do so in the future. At the same time there is no denying that it makes for some very acute difficulties. For instance, we have a tremendous need for more schools and more teachers. Transportation in populous areas is already in critical shape. Municipal and town boundaries laid out years ago are out of date so that we have a confusion of local governments.

5. We have a profound need to make industry more productive. This is the only way I know to combat the pressures of inflation. Certainly we shall have to turn out more goods in order to maintain, let alone improve, standards of living for a larger population. At the same time there is no prospect that we can now count on to reduce the high costs of defense. To pay these costs yet raise living standards, capital must be used in more productive ways.

6. We need a better relationship between industry and government than we now have. This is neither the time nor the place to debate a position and I don't intend to do so. I am simply trying to state an objective fact. This is that we must have a dynamic, expanding economy, our position in the world depends on it, and to achieve it people in industry and people in government must work together and not at odds with each other. I know of course that sincere and devoted individuals in both fields are doing their utmost, and I am sure too that they are in the majority. But we need the most understanding and co-operation that can be achieved, and that is something more than we have now.

I spoke of the using up of our natural resources. The time is coming when we shall need new sources for necessities that we cannot import. One is water, as I am sure you are well aware. Another is energy. How to draw fresh water economically from the sea, how to find the best ways to make liquid fuels from coal, and how to use efficiently the power of the atom and the sun.

These are challenges of vital importance and absorbing interest.

I spoke also of growing population. Some scientists consider this the great world problem of the next hundred years. They recognize, of course, that long-range forecasts cannot be made with assurance. Still, the number of human beings is increasing faster than ever before. Death rates have fallen throughout the world, while birth rates have not gone down to match. In so-called undeveloped or underdeveloped countries, more and more people, under present conditions, will tend to get less and less nourishment. As I understand it, history shows that birth rates have fallen only in countries which have had a high degree of industrial development, with all the improvement in education, standards of living, and general culture that go along with economic progress. This seems to say that unless underdeveloped countries are able to make substantial industrial and economic gains in the next century, world population may get out of hand.

So every day from here on out, great and decisive events are surely in the making. And for you the real question is: will your brains and energy be a part of their making—or will you watch them on TV?

A Manly Spirit

One Sunday last fall, not long after the Russians had sent up their first Sputnik, I was impressed by the sermon my pastor preached. His message was simple. He said he thought we had need in this country for a more manly spirit. Many Americans, he said, seemed deeply affected and easily thrown off balance by rumors and half-truths. We were so sure of ourselves on the surface, in an adolescent sort of way, so confident that we can do everything better than anybody else, and yet so easily excited or disturbed. And he suggested that perhaps a reason for this may be that we are too little concerned with things of real value, and too much absorbed in matters of little consequence; whereas if a man's mind and heart are deeply engaged in the vital affairs and problems he shares with others, he will not tip over in every breeze. And so the preacher appealed for a spirit that is studious, thorough, responsible, mature, that willingly accepts personal involvement in the issues of our time, and which he called, to embrace all these qualities, a manly spirit.

Please note that one of the qualities he named was studiousness. One reason why this is so important is that the rate of change in the world is so much faster than it used to be. The mind that stays still today, in a very little while will fall hopelessly behind. Many of you are engineers. I can assure you that in a few years, the technology you will be working in will be remarkably different from what you will be doing on your first job. And for all of you, whether you are engineers or not, the impact of change will be very strong. It will be so strong that you will be glad of every effort you have made to keep your mind clear and to dig your understanding deep.

To be studious, I think, is something more than to study books, though I certainly wouldn't advise you to leave that out. It is also to study the content of a job, and the ways of getting it accomplished. It is to study people as well as tools. It is to know the affairs of one's city or town, and qualify oneself for the duties of being a citizen. It is to be self-critical, and ask oneself how others accomplish what you may find difficult to do. It is to think about personal goals, and thoughtfully decide whether they are sound and good, from the standpoint of others as well as from your own. It is to set one's mind on growth, and to explore all things that will help to achieve it; to be determined to be one's full self, and competent to make the whole contribution which your conscience tells you may rightly be expected.

It seems to me that this approach to living is at the opposite pole from the idea that a man should devote himself primarily or exclusively to reaching a comfortable security. Let me say just a little about that word security. I don't underestimate its importance. Of course people want to feel reasonably secure. When you marry you will want to provide for your family and that is your obligation. As a nation we are deeply engaged to maintain and secure our freedom. We recognize the need for what has come to be called social security. Business organizations, no less than government, have been trying more and more to minimize job insecurity. In still another aspect, we know that the emotional sense of security and confidence in others has a great deal to do with good mental health.

In fact, part of what we mean when we speak of raising standards of living is that we want to increase security and decrease insecurity. But I do not think we shall accomplish this if we begin with the idea of making cozy nooks for ourselves. That is not a very lofty goal, and the people who have that sort of goal are really leaving the responsibilities of leadership to others. Equally, whether they know it or not, they are missing the real zest of life, and its best rewards.

I am only saying that the best security comes from the kind of studiousness I have tried to describe, and from the constant practice of one's talents and abilities. The man who makes sure of his powers, who really will go as far as he can to develop himself, is likely to be the man who in the long run will be most secure and serene notwithstanding adversity. If we should all dedicate ourselves to small conceptions of personal security, I think we would wind up with a very flimsy and unstable society. But if we take the other way, with more concern for our capacities and less for our comfort, then I am sure we shall be doing the most to create real security for the nation and also for ourselves.

KNOX COLLEGE

JUNE 1, 1959

No more than anything else can freedom stand still; it will either grow or wither. And even in less critical times, making democracy work has been a difficult and delicate matter. For freedom encourages differences of all kinds; differences of ideas, of tastes, of ambitions, of personal goals. We don't want to be shaped or formed according to some standard model. We want to disagree and argue with each other. We insist that what is good for Tom is not thereby also good for Harry. We stand on our rights and stick up for our opinions. We want the air of freedom and we don't want it air-conditioned by somebody else.

These are fine principles and they lead us into many kinds of good. The competition of people who feel themselves free puts a tremendous energy to work. We are invigorated and encouraged to explore, invent, and innovate. By pursuing different goals we get a rich variety of results. And the process of debate opens our minds to the ideas of others. The give and take of freedom stirs up thinking and uncovers talents that would otherwise never come to life.

However, freedom can also bring bad results. We can become absorbed in seeking personal advantage. We can focus on our rights to the exclusion of most other things. We can listen to what we like to hear, and shut our ears to the rest. We can come to think that because we are free, we shall not be held to account. Worst of all (and this sums up the bad news in six words) we can take freedom for granted.

So I think it comes down to this—that this difficult and delicate business of making democracy work depends on the quality of individual lives, and on how they nourish each other. It depends on people developing themselves with the idea of contributing something, and not just taking something. It depends on their eagerness to exercise their personal talents, and their personal tastes, in ways that enrich the common life. It depends on their interest in helping to bring out the best in other people. It depends on vigorous and thoughtful participation in political life. It depends on capacity for self-discipline—by which I do not at all mean a merely stern or puritanical discipline, but the kind of discipline that people with worthwhile goals happily impose on themselves.

You may ask: are not people inherently disposed to look out for themselves? Aren't they motivated by the desire for material rewards? And in business, to be specific, isn't it the drive for profit that generates economic progress?

These are fair questions and the straight answer to them is yes. Certainly the pulls of self-interest are very strong. And they do contribute to social gains. Of course they do. If men and women had never wanted to better their lot, we'd still be throwing spears to get food. But civilized people have to temper self-interest. It is not enough for them. They need something more, and so does civilized society if it is to remain civilized. We have to have an educated, intelligent, thoughtful balance of interest; regard for other people as individuals; personal concern for the common welfare; devotion, and I will say dedication, to something beyond ourselves.

Three Suggestions

Aside from these broad comments, there are three fairly specific things I had in mind suggesting to you.

One has to do with quality of workmanship. And if you don't mind, I'll use one or two examples drawn from the communications business to help illustrate the point.

A few weeks ago one of my associates was telling about the results of a missile test shot over the South Atlantic. This was the first time the nose cone of a long-range missile had been recovered. Since the system for guiding the missile had been designed at our Bell Telephone Laboratories, you can see that we were particularly interested.

Measuring the position and speed of the missile in flight, the guidance system was able to calculate with pinpoint accuracy just where the nose cone would fall in the sea, five thousand miles away.

Let me give you two or three figures to indicate what this means. When the rocket engine cuts off, the speed of the missile out in space is around twenty-four thousand feet per second. But a variation of *one* foot per second at the cutoff point will cause a difference of about a mile in where the nose cone lands. So you see how remarkably accurate the guidance system must be.

The second example relates to the new transoceanic telephone cables we have been building in recent years. To make these work, we have to have electronic amplifiers every forty miles or so at the bottom of the sea. If any one of the amplifiers should fail, then the cable has to be raised and a new amplifier spliced in. This is a difficult and costly operation, and most important, service over the cable is interrupted until the repairs have been made. So we have designed and built our amplifiers with the greatest care. We have tested every component to the limit. The work-space in which they are assembled is kept under a slight air pressure to exclude any possible dust. Employees wear special lint-free clothing. They have their shoes shined before they enter the shop. I recall that for certain parts in each amplifier we have to wind about fifteen hundred feet of fine wire which is only one and a half thousandths of an inch thick. Every inch of this wiring is carefully examined under a microscope.

The point is simply this: To get important things done, we *do* have to strive for perfection. To my mind this is not just talk. I think it is a fact. Nor can we say that while this may be true in solving technical problems, it is not so true in other fields of effort. The human problems are the hardest of all, and all the more so because we cannot measure results, or discover mistakes, with a ruler or a stop watch. It is not easy to do a good job—ever. But I do not believe this will dismay you.

The second thought I have is somewhat related to what I

have just been saying. Good jobs cannot be accomplished by rule or by rote. In the last couple of years or so I have heard quite a bit about somebody called the Organization Man. I am not exactly sure who he is, but I think he exists, and I think one of his characteristics is that he is more concerned with avoiding pitfalls than with blazing trails. The fault for this may well be his, but it may also be the organization's for encouraging him in his error. If this is so, it means that to avoid making little mistakes, the organization man and the organization collaborate to make a big one.

I am afraid the reputation of the organization man has promoted the idea that in big companies a few people do the thinking and a lot of other people behave accordingly. I wouldn't say to you that this is never so. I do say there is no good reason under heaven why it should be so, and that where it is, it will not be so for long, for under these conditions the organization is not fitting itself to survive.

The fact is, the business of a big organization calls for thousands of individual decisions and these must be made by thousands of people. Moreover these individual decisions are not petty. They are very influential. And it is only by reason of these decisions that the organization moves and acts. It cannot move as a solid mass. That is simply impossible. A business is not a glacier.

Any organization you enter will in some way put its mark on you. However you live and work will show on you. But the symphonies of Beethoven are no less personal expressions because they are recognizably German. In the same way, the kind of music you make will have a certain character that reflects your environment, but this does not at all mean you can't give it the distinctive personal quality that comes only from you.

My last suggestion has to do with politics. I hope some of you will go into politics and I hope all of you will take politics seriously. The Greeks may not have a word for you and me, but the politicians do have one. We are their constituents. And as they face up to decisions, they all the time have to be thinking about what *we* are thinking.

Certainly they have both the opportunity and responsibility

for leadership. Nor should we make the mistake of underestimating their capacity for independent thinking. Nevertheless, legislators in a democratic country face a very, very difficult problem. They cannot dissociate themselves from the views of their constituents and hope to remain in office. But what are our views? And how thoughtful are they? If they are narrow and provincial, and do not take into account the serious problems that confront the whole country, then our lawmakers have no help in making crucial decisions that affect the welfare of all. In plain language, if *we* think small, how can we expect *them* to act big?

Furthermore, if we think well and broadly, but still are silent, what are we contributing then? Nothing at all, it seems to me. So I urge you not only to think as big as you can, but to know and communicate with your elected representatives. To ponder the questions they are wrestling with. To express your views to them, not hastily or carelessly, but on the basis of care and conviction. To be as active as you can be in party affairs and in political campaigns.

UNION COLLEGE

JUNE 14, 1959

As I read the comments and observations of men who look at our national life from very different points of view, it seems to me there is one thought often repeated. This is the disturbing thought that the interests of groups are standing in the way of our national interests.

The liberal may say it one way and the conservative another. The businessman, the educator, the economist, the union leader, and the man in public life all speak with different voices and in different tones; some objectively and some with heat. But again and again, this thought is repeated: We are putting personal and private interests first. We are prevented from doing things that would serve everyone well, because they come into conflict with the interests of groups that have power to prevent them. We are losing chance after chance to promote the welfare of all because we continually compromise and commit ourselves to meet the wishes of a few.

These are uncomfortable thoughts. However, I am glad to hear them said. I am glad because I hope that to hear them will rouse our minds and stir our energies. I hope it will spur us to understand better what our common interests are, and how overwhelmingly important they are, and jolt us into working more devotedly to advance them.

Some people say that much of our trouble is due to the fact that our form of government doesn't focus enough authority in any one place. That may be part of it, though I doubt that putting more authority in this spot or that would ever be a cure-all. Others seem to think that private individuals just can't be trusted to want what is good for society, so government ought to decide most everything; and with that I can't agree at all. Nor do I think we can simply pass the buck to our political leaders, and then put all the blame for our failures on them. Unity is not just a game of follow the leader. Real unity of purpose comes from people themselves reaching out and coming to reasonable agreement on what it is they want together.

What It Means to Be Yourself

Let's consider a phrase we all know and use. "Be yourself"—those are the words I mean. Put them together and they dig hard at every one of us. Sometimes you may say them to get a person to relax. Or to ask somebody who is putting on airs to climb down off his horse. However, the same words can also go much deeper.

Be yourself. That means, I think, explore and discover yourself; test out your boundaries; see if they will stretch a little. It means, nourish and exercise whatever you find within yourself that seems most hopeful and promising to you. It means, don't accept without thinking, don't follow blindly. It means, learn what you can take, for otherwise it will be hard indeed to discover what you can do.

Now I'll go back a moment to what I was saying earlier. That we need a wider and deeper sharing of purpose in this country. That we need to work for unity, with greater dedication to the common welfare. Are those thoughts inconsistent with this emphasis on being yourself?

I do not think so. For if we do not go deep into ourselves, I doubt that we can share deeply with others. If we do not broaden our personal boundaries, we shall hardly see far enough to perceive what the common welfare may be, let alone work to advance it. In fact, it seems to me it is only if we make the effort to be ourselves—our full selves—that we can successfully live and work together as a united free people and nation. For as I see it, this intense personal effort is essential to develop, on the one hand, the great diversity of brains and talent we require, and on the other hand, real understanding of our mutual interests.

Now I assume some of you, though doubtless not all, are

planning to go into business. And as I have talked about exploring and developing yourself, and being yourself, you may have been wondering how that squares with some of the things you have heard about people in business, particularly big business. I think you know what I am talking about: it is the idea that a man becomes just a part of the organization; that he becomes so much a member of a group that he ceases to be himself.

Well, this can happen and does happen—sometimes. But there are also a few other things to say about it. One is that when it does occur, the organization is just as bothered by it as the individual is, and frequently a good deal more so. I would say too that if a man makes a compromise with himself when he goes into an organization, in so doing he is stacking the cards the wrong way. By compromise I mean for example this: that what he puts first in his mind is "a good steady job"; that what he is after is an unexhilarating lifetime security, all neatly arranged with regular vacations, and every weekend free for do-it-yourself projects down in the basement. If this is the way he thinks, then he is what I would call an organization man before he joins the organization.

To those who are going into business I shall simply say: Please don't follow this mirage. Please don't accept this philosophy from anyone. Business really isn't looking for people who make this kind of projection ahead. And as educated men, you can't do this and be yourselves.

Is there room for individuality in big business? Is there real opportunity for the exercise of personal freedom? You bet there is. Sometimes I am asked how it is, for example, that the Bell System is able to conduct basic scientific research that gets results. Being a business, don't we bend the scientists' minds this way or that, and thereby impede their efforts? The answer is precisely that we go on the principle that we will not bend them at all. If we did, they would not work for us.

It puzzles me that people will readily accept this answer as to science and research, yet fail to comprehend that a business is just as anxious to foster creativeness in other fields as well. The fact is that many companies are working hard to build the kind of environment that favors the individual's will to grow. And to say just a word more from our own experience, we believe that in the Bell System we have learned quite a bit about what it takes to do this.

First, as I have indicated, a man must be free to grow in his own best way—not along the lines of some standard model.

Second, when his further growth requires a new challenge, it must be presented to him without delay.

Third, it requires the opportunity to take on real responsibility, and to taste the fruits of failure, sometimes, as well as success.

Fourth, it takes rewards for being bold and imaginative—for being creative—for exercising judgment.

Finally, it takes exposure to the world outside the business. And it seems to us that both the company and the man are jointly responsible for making sure that he does not escape this exposure. So we try to open up many approaches to the broadening of minds—through conference study and discussion of many kinds of problems, through planned reading, and through seminars and courses both inside the business and in the universities, not only in technical and business subjects, but also in the social sciences and sometimes in the arts.

All this is pointed at doing our job in the world as well and effectively as we can, and as much to the advantage of the country as we can. But this depends on having people who want to grow—to be themselves.

OHIO WESLEYAN UNIVERSITY

JUNE 5, 1960

So far as I know, every contribution ever made to the progress of civilization has come about because individual people developed themselves and generated ideas and practiced talents and then turned their ideas and talents to account. Often the ultimate achievement may be the work of groups. But everything we cherish had its start in some one person's mind, some one person's hand, some one person's heart.

If this seems reasonable to you, I'll go on to three points that seem to me to have important bearing on individual development.

First, I am sure one of the main efforts of your teachers here in college has been to help you develop an inquiring, thoughtful turn of mind. I share their hope that before you accept ideas, you will question them first. I hope it will always be your habit to challenge, examine, and analyze. Naturally, as time goes on your thinking will lead to certain conclusions and even convictions. But the point is to reach them on the basis of your own observation and reasoning, rather than carry around a set of ideas that are carbon copies of somebody else's.

This has always been the mark of the individual, and I suppose I am only repeating here what many other commencement speakers have said in other years. One reason for saying it again is that there has never been a time when people were so flooded by other people's words. Newspapers, magazines, radio, and TV pour them out by the million. Great drifts of information and misinformation pile up all around us. Ideas are merchandised like soap, a lot of the soap is soft, and nonsense gets more mileage than it deserves. Discrimination in reading and listening, therefore, is absolutely essential. If we are not discriminating as to the ideas we take in, the ideas we give out will have no great merit either.

Second, a few words about the individual and organizations. The gist of my comment is this: You certainly *can* belong to an organization and still be your unique self, if you will be. Moreover your individual character and abilities are precisely what any organization you have a hand in most needs and wants from you.

Please don't fear organization. Organization is necessary to get things done. It always has been. I suspect that many people nowadays wish we could find ways to unwind large organizations and get back to simpler modes of living. But this is impossible. Modern life has to be highly organized. Otherwise we cannot support our population, maintain our national security, educate our children, aid other countries, and discover and use wisely the resources that will be necessary to life in future generations.

The true individualist has nothing to fear from organization and a great deal to gain. Much of what you accomplish in life, and many of your satisfactions, will come through participating in organized activities. I'm not talking just about business. I'm talking about all sorts of organizations: P.T.A. groups, home owners' associations, service clubs, social agencies, churches, women's auxiliaries, industry associations, professional societies, political parties. For many years, voluntary participation in organizations has been one of the distinguishing characteristics of American life, and it has had great and good influence on our social progress.

As I see it, the growth of organized activity simply *increases* the need for vital, independent, strong-minded people who are trying to develop their unique capacities to the utmost. No organized effort can long succeed, or even move in the right direction, except as able individuals make their highly personal and distinctive contributions to it.

The Necessity for Self-Development

The third point is that there is only one person who can develop your capabilities, and that is you yourself. This is your responsibility and it cannot be anyone else's. Those of you who are starting out on free-lance careers, so to speak, and you girls who are going straight from college to matrimony, are no doubt clear on this already. Maybe you all are. But particularly for those who are joining some organization, what I have to say here may save you from a misapprehension:

Many organizations today put a lot of emphasis on the training young people will get *after* they go to work. It is possible therefore for the idea to get around that the first years of a working career will be something like a continuation of college. And this is just not so. It is not so at all. There is a big difference and you should know it before you start.

All through your education, the main activity at the schools you have attended has been directed at one goal, namely, your development. This is what schools are for. But from now on, unless you go to a graduate school, the main purpose of the people you will be working with will not be to educate you. Their main purpose will be to carry on a business, or administer some public office, or teach other people, or heal the sick, or run a farm, or whatnot. If you should chance to be described temporarily as a "trainee" or a "student," please don't let the word deceive you. Your training will be a very important concern of your associates, sure enough. But I repeat, it cannot be their main concern, their principal goal. That will always be to get work done and done well.

Furthermore, no matter how much training you receive, no matter how much other people help you, no matter what things are put in your way to stimulate your mind and nourish your growth, none of this can ever take over your development as a person. Only you can develop your own powers. Only you can be your own prime mover. Simple as this may sound, still it is the most demanding thing that I can say to you, and I think the most important.

RENSSELAER POLYTECHNIC INSTITUTE

JUNE 9, 1961

ONE troublesome thing about the future is that we have no facts about it. But scientists, engineers, architects, and managers are endlessly concerned with the future and to a large degree they are responsible for it. For example, their insights and judgments largely determine how investment capital, the foundation of our economic system, shall be invested. This is a tremendous responsibility. Since you came to Rensselaer, business firms have spent about a hundred and seventy billion dollars for new equipment and buildings installed or erected in this country, and residential construction has totaled another seventy-five billion dollars or more. Have these vast sums been spent wisely? Every dollar was paid out according to the judgments of individual minds. Were the judgments penetrating and sound? This is a crucial question and for the answer each individual is personally accountable.

I ask you also to mark this: We might take a limited view of the accountability and say that the money was wisely spent if it enabled us to realize the goals we had in mind in the most effective way possible. But is this really the whole story? We know it is not. The basic question is—did we have the right goals in the first place?

In other words, how well we are able to finish depends on how well we are able to begin. Not that a good start assures a good ending, far from it. But if we fail in our first steps, each subsequent step will only take us further astray. The first challenge to judgment is not, "Am I tackling this problem in the right way?" The first challenge is, "What *is* the problem? Does the problem or the opportunity exist at all? What is the need? What is wanted? Is this what I ought to be doing?"

I am saying here that good technical or engineering decisions cannot be based on purely technical or engineering considerations. If it is a matter of introducing a new product or service, it is first of all a matter of knowing what people need and want. If it is a matter of aid to Laos, or any other country, it is likewise and absolutely a matter of knowing as well as possible what is truly needed and wanted. And it is precisely because, as I have said, there are no facts about the future, that the technical expert cannot rely on his technical expertness, or the theorist get married to his theory. Technique and theory are indispensable, but we have to test them constantly and rigorously in the disconcerting glare of experience. Furthermore what is measurable and scientific is everlastingly snarled up with the unmeasurable and human, so in order to test his judgments well the scientist, the architect, or the engineer has no recourse except to stir into his particular pot of understanding every last thing he can learn about economics, public taste, tribal customs, social problems, national goals, the peculiarities of politics, and the aims, quirks, and foibles of people generally. No more than a surgeon can operate by reading a book, or an economist manage a budget by quoting from his own works, can you depend on your slide rule to ask the right questions or get the right answers.

A related point, I am convinced, is that the direction technological change is taking will require more and more that what you do be unique—that is, that the work you perform should represent a unique contribution that cannot be duplicated. The reason for this is simple. Computers can compute far better than people can. Therefore people whose only talent is to make more or less routine calculations will not be needed for that purpose.

When I say you will be called on for unique contributions, I do not mean that your destiny henceforth must be to come up with eccentric inventions. I mean simply that your judgment, your imagination, your sensitivity to the life around you, your perception of what the problem is and how to attack it—these are the major factors that will distinguish your professional achievement.

These and courage also, because after all the available facts are assembled and all the data evaluated, they will still not add up to the answer. It is you who must decide, and in so doing risk your reputation and career. Furthermore the qualities I have mentioned will be just as necessary to your achievement in a large organization as in a small one, or as they will be if you are your own boss.

So we have the need, first, to discover what the problem or opportunity is, to ask the right questions, to find out what our goals should be. We have the need to develop our understanding of human wants. We have the need to put theories rigorously to the test before we attempt to launch them in practice. We have the need to summon all the imagination and creativity of which we are capable in order to accomplish our particular and personal tasks.

How far from being technological can a technological change be? Let me illustrate rather hastily by an example from the communications business. We are now creating the first stages of a data communication network, over which, as the layman puts it, machines will talk to machines. Already it appears that the impact will go far beyond getting work done faster, more efficiently, and at lower cost. We foresee that this development will permit entirely new forms of business organization. Both industry and government will be able to conduct widely decentralized operations under circumstances that permit extremely fast and accurate centralized control. Where offices and plants will be located, where people will live and how they will work, all such factors may be radically altered.

But no company, no organization, no government, can wisely organize its own change unless and until it thoroughly understands itself, its goals, the hazards ahead, the needs of people. Thus technological advance puts us all to the test. It puts a premium on thoughtful judgment; on ability to choose among alternatives; on the talent for seeing relationships that less perceptive minds will miss. In sum, it demands the hardest of all human accomplishments, which is merely to have wisdom. And this I may remind you is more than a matter of brains. It is a moral achievement. Wisdom and ethical conduct cannot be separated. No matter what your abilities, their value to you and to others will always be determined by your character, your respect for your fellow men, your sense of right and wrong.

MICHIGAN STATE UNIVERSITY

JUNE 9, 1963

To be lively and vital, to act with enthusiasm and imagination, business needs reasonable freedom. It needs room to move around in. It needs the latitude to cut and try. I am sure you have this need for freedom and the people in a business are just like you.

But to keep its freedom, business, again just like any individual, must everlastingly show its competence and responsibility. If it doesn't, then sure as shooting the community, the public, the government, will tie it down, curb and control it, limit and reduce its fields of opportunity, and more and more take over functions that business now performs.

I think this would be a calamity and I don't believe it is only those of us in business who have this view.

I know there are some people—I believe a small minority—who want to see more and more state control. But that is not the feeling of most of the people I know in government and in the universities, and I know a good many.

Just consider two points:

First, the tasks of government are hard enough as they are. Government has always been the most difficult, the most exacting problem of mankind. This was true when life was relatively simple, and the job is much harder today when human affairs have become so much more complex. It is a harder and bigger job; inevitably there is more for government to do today than in the past. And government is finding it mighty tough to cope with all the new problems that spring up every year. It isn't any accident that we hear so many questions raised as to whether the machinery of government, the forms of organization that have existed for years, the procedures that have become established, are really adequate to enable legislators, for example, to handle their tasks effectively.

I conclude, therefore, that if government already has all the balls in the air that it can handle, then it is only common sense for government not to try to do things it could better leave to others—I mean, to you and me as individuals, and to private organizations and enterprises of many kinds.

Especially (and this is the second point) when the people of this country have shown an initiative, an inventiveness, an ability to drive ahead through the private enterprise system, that have set the pace for the world.

The basic value of private enterprise to my notion is that it does challenge the individual hard. It offers rewards but it demands risk. It measures performance in a setting of continuous, never-ending competition. It invites pluralistic, rather than monolithic, effort—that is, it gets people to start attacking diverse problems in individual, personal ways. This challenge to the free individual in my belief has been the principal source of economic progress in this country, and for it I can see no really effective substitute.

I have a few comments also regarding scholarship and teaching in economics and other fields related to business, government, and economic life generally.

It seems to me the educators in these fields have a particularly challenging assignment.

Where Knowledge of Business Comes From

One reason for this is that the main source of knowledge about modern business is *in* business. It is not in the schools. Consequently, the study of business is rather different from the study of Greek, or medieval history, or Shakespeare. It is different also from a field like medicine where so many new developments emanate from university medical centers. In business, most of the learning, most of the new developments, most of the steps forward come out of business itself. And the pace of change is mighty fast.

Hence scholarship in the field needs a large component of

knowledge based on first-hand, intimate acquaintance with business problems as they emerge in the heat of the day.

At the same time, the scholar's need for thoughtful evaluation requires that he keep himself in the position of being able to see the forest and not just a few trees.

These two requirements make his task, as I said, particularly difficult.

It is with full awareness of this that I now make a businessman's plea to the professors, and likewise to those of you who look forward to being scholars and teachers in this field. My plea is simply that you do all you can to make sure that your facts always march ahead of your conclusions.

Some professors, I am told, take a dim view of the average businessman's understanding of economics. My own impression is that there is a fair supply of academic economists who have very little intuitive understanding of real-life business affairs. I have a deep respect for the abilities of men who can master economic theory. However, I sometimes wish that some of them would be a little more inclined to take seriously certain practical problems that seem very important to me. But without prolonging my argument, I will just say again that when the scholar moves into the area of devising solutions for practical problems, I hope his scholarship will encompass all the effort he can devote to studying and knowing the problems at first hand.

We need a full and free exchange of views between business managers and academic people. I remember one professor saying to me, after he had had a session with a Bell System group, that he didn't know who had done more learning, they or he. I am sure he was being modest but I was delighted by the comment because it meant there had been communication both ways and that is so much needed. As I have indicated, I do believe that we in business have something to communicate to the academic community. On the other hand, we know full well that university people have a great deal to offer us not only in imparting knowledge, but in the questions they ask, their ability to make us aware of considerations we might otherwise miss, and their power also to help us get a new vision of familiar things.

INDEX

INDEX